Sisters in Sin

The Nellie Spencer Story

By
Duane A. Smith

WESTERN REFLECTIONS PUBLISHING COMPANY®

ISBN 978-1-932738-95-7

Library of Congress Control Number: 2011921641

Cover and text design: Steve Smith, FluiDESIGNS

First Edition
Printed in the United States of America

Western Reflections Publishing Company™
P.O. Box 1149
951 N. Highway 149
Lake City, CO 81235
www.westernreflectionspublishing.com

For the Class of 1955
Sandwich Township High School

Table of Contents

Preface . . . . *i*
   Nellie

Prologue . . . . *v*
   Prostitution

Chapter 1 . . . . *1*
   Rush to the San Juans: Urbanization Arrives

Chapter 2 . . . . *17*
   City Revenue Source or Sinful Pleasure?

Chapter 3 . . . . *33*
   Working the Line: Prostitution in the San Juans, 1870s-1890s

Chapter 4 . . . . *47*
   Times They Are A Changing: Prostitution in the San Juans, 1890s-
   1900s

Chapter 5 . . . . *65*
   Nellie's Story

Chapter 6 . . . . *73*
   Working Girl

Chapter 7 . . . . *101*
   Nellie's Friends and Acquaintances, As They Knew Her

Chapter 8 . . . . *119*
   Nellie, Bessie, and Friends: Durango's Queens of the Tenderloin

Epilogue *139*
   Requiem for Prostitution

Index *147*

Preface
Nellie

Nellie Spencer was an amazing survivor. From her childhood to her senior years, she persevered against odds that might have sunk a less determined and survivor-oriented individual.

I waited a long time to interview her and finally had the pleasure of spending many sessions with Nellie over the course of a couple of years in the early 1980s. She may have been hard of hearing and blind in one eye, but she possessed a good memory of her life and her days on "the line."

Her story is worth repeating; it is the story of an indomitable woman who survived and prospered in the world of prostitution. It has been said that it is a basic human instinct to make something of oneself monetarily or in some other manner. This drive, of course, can take one beyond a socially acceptable point. There are checks to this. As it has been written, "capitalism is to greed, what marriage is to lust." Nellie managed to survive and break the mold in both instances. In her case, Shakespeare was correct when he wrote, "some rise by sin, and some by virtue fall."

Nellie coped in this world very well, very well indeed. She proved to be good in her profession as was shown by the statement that during the World War I era and the 1920s she earned $100 for an "over night." That represented good money for sex during a time when $5, $10 or occasionally $20 for a trick proved much more common. Much to the dismay of reformers, "sin is profitable."

No doubt, many, probably the vast majority of people in Nellie's day, thought her occupation as sinful. Discussing "sin," Mark Twain put his finger on the matter. "One could. . . say that God is the personage who should shoulder the blame for sin that is in the world (& suffer the punishment) because He made sin attractive & put it in the reach of the sinner."

The reader will find some repetition in the questions in this book and in Nellie's answers. The former was, on my part, a small attempt at cross checking her memory. On Nellie's part, it was her age or the fact that she sometimes wanted to expand on an answer, or answers, that she had given previously. All these have been left in the text without editing and the same holds true for the other interviews quoted.

The reader may also wonder, why study prostitution and interview one of the participants? Mabel Barbee Lee in her *Cripple Creek Days* described her feelings toward the lovely Pearl DeVere, "… but even I, an eleven-year schoolgirl, knew that it wasn't her right name."

> People said she came of a good family in the East who believed that she was a high-toned dressmaker—the designer of 'De Vere Gowns' for the wives of Cripple Creek's millionaires. Actually she was the madam at the camp's fanciest sporting house, the Old Homestead on Myers Avenue.
>
> Once in a breathless instant when I was staring at her from around a telegraph pole, she glanced down and smiled at me. I was spellbound; never had I laid eyes on

such an enchanting vision! From that day, Pearl De Vere became my secret sorrow, the heroine of my fondest daydreams, mysterious, fascinating and forbidden.

I was more interested in what went on at the Old Homestead, and speculated endlessly about it. But my rangy musings got me nowhere and I was afraid to ask questions of grownups.

Young Mabel Barbee's fascination echoes down the decades. So, unfortunately, has the image of the beautiful, happy, fun-loving prostitute.

Anne Butler in her classic study, *Daughters of Joy, Sisters of Misery: Prostitutes in the American West, 1865-1890,* answered that question in a more scholarly manner.

It is unsettling that, while curiosity about prostitutes has never been scarce, society's fascination has been marked by a prurient tilt toward sensational erotica and moralistic judgments. As a consequence our historical understanding of this worldwide, long-established institution has remained incomplete for many years.

More recently, research trends have encouraged scholars to turn their attention to the less notable or seemingly unimportant groups in society. Prostitutes fall naturally into this category. Scholars now recognize that in many cultures, across a wide sweep of time, prostitutes represented an important societal ingredient. From a variety of scholarly persuasions, a growing body of literature closes the gap between mythical nonsense and orderly knowledge.

This volume hopefully will help to better explain reality and perhaps end some of the enduring myths about the "fair but frail."

Given the often sensational writing about prostitutes and prostitution, the author concurs completely with the comments made by Jan MacKell in her *Brothels, Bordellos, & Bad Girls*.

> The intention of this book is not to romanticize, poke fun at, or degrade long-departed prostitutes of Colorado. It is not meant to point fingers, accuse, or reveal embarrassing information. Rather, I have chosen to recognize one of society's most unappreciated and misunderstood classes…

She concluded, "no matter its legalities, prostitution was in demand and flourished wherever men were willing to pay for it."

The author owes a debt of thanks to many people whose names are found in the text, along with those who preferred not to be identified. They were gracious enough to speak to me about Nellie, some of the other "erring sisters" of the time, or Durango's red light district. My whole family was involved in this project, as were my good friends Bob Hill, James Erickson, and Suzanne Peterson, and Tom Doak.

Prologue
Prostitution

There is an old doggerel from the days of the California gold rush, "The miners came in '49, the whores in '51, and when they got together, they produced the native son." It would be just as truthful and easy to substitute '59 and '61 for the Pike's Peak gold rush.

In the nineteenth century, in the American West's mining towns and camps, the saloons, dance halls, and bordellos emerged as the social center for many unattached young men. In these places they found male and female companionship that could not be obtained anywhere else for many of them. And so, prostitution became a notable trade in the San Juans, Colorado, and throughout the West. In fact, in the male-dominated mining West, the red light district could be the men's only chance to escape, if only briefly, the male world around them. Linda Wommack, in her book *The Ladies of the Tenderloin*, summarized the prostitute's role in this world.

> The prostitution influence in the West was a direct reflection of the lack of women in the region. By this

very virtue, prostitutes were a needed and desired commodity. The fact that prostitution remained a viable commodity, despite the later presence of women of moral virtue, speaks more to Victorian platitudes than to the prostitutes of the West.

Before going further, it must be kept clearly in mind, that the overwhelmingly vast majority of the women in the West were not "soiled doves" or involved in any way with the profession. They were wives and mothers, whose main effort was establishing and maintaining homes and rearing their children. They also quite often led the fight against the red light district and its inhabitants.

The red light district and prostitution were part and parcel of the Colorado mining era. Unlike their agrarian contemporaries throughout the country, early Colorado pioneers urbanized from the very first, settling into camps and towns nestled near the mines. It was a masculine dominated world. In theory, the prospectors and miners had money, and the majority of them were single. The predictable development resulted in a pattern seen through the West. In came the "ladies of the line, the erring sisters, the fair but frail, the women of the town," or whatever soubriquet they might be called, to "mine the miners," as the saying went.

Despite legend and fiction, prostitution was not a glamorous profession, even if some call it the "second oldest profession," and a few have called it the "oldest profession." The red light district—saloons, parlor houses, cribs, gambling "hells," and low-class variety theaters— was the center of crime, social diseases, loneliness, fallen hopes, lost dreams, physical and mental abuse of women, drugs, alcoholism, and desperation. It was not the kind of place that often appears in stories about the line and the girls who occupied it. Somehow, over time, it has evolved as a generally romantic part of the "real" West, a glamorized institution in a glorified epoch. It was anything but that in the reality of that era.

Telluride Madam
Homer Reid Collection

Nor were the women as beautiful as has often been portrayed in movies and on television. The vast majorities were not as pretty as Miss Kitty, in the long running "Gunsmoke" television series, nor were the saloons, for that matter, like the Long Branch. The slim, trim woman was not fashionable, for no other reason than plumpness was socially and stylistically "in" for women during this age. Nor were there many older women involved, as prostitution usually wore down its participants at a relatively early age.

Why then would women enter this degrading, "dead-end" profession? That question has been raised, probed, and examined over the centuries, with varying results. No one reason predominates and indeed, it may be said to vary over the years. The answer seems to depend upon the individual.

Desire for easy money, bad relationships, love, and excitement are frequently mentioned. Also, abandonment and unfaithfulness by a husband or a "special friend" appear to rise to the surface, particularly in the transitory life that surrounded mining and mining communities. Economic troubles or lack of occupational skills drove some women into prostitution, as did broken and cheerless homes. Some women, no doubt, enjoyed the life style or found it an easy way to procure drugs—or whatever they sought or hoped to gain. Regardless of the reason, Nellie and her cohorts probably rarely found it to be a completely satisfying situation or condition of life. Obviously the reverse held true as they eventually found out.

Still, prostitution flourished as a part of the mining West and certainly in Colorado's mining days. It caught the attention of tourists of that day and of writers and romantics since. Some became fascinated, others were repelled, but the prostitution district and its inhabitants could not be ignored.

Frank Fossett, writing in his 1878 edition of *Colorado*, reflected favorably upon the prostitutes.

> To the abandoned and fallen women, who followed the army of prospectors, like a swarm of locusts, some credit is due. Wretched and degraded, ignored by the Christian, and spat upon by the so-called moralist, victims of a jeering world, they forgot "Man's inhumanity to man," and were the direct means of saving many valuable lives from that dreaded disease, mountain fever.

Similar comments were made by others who lived in or visited the various Colorado communities and mining districts of the time.

The districts and the girls held the fascination of youngsters in the camps and towns, much to their parents' disapproval. Ellen Jacobson grew up in Telluride when the town reached its peak of prosperity in the early part of the twentieth century. She remembered the red light district through the eyes of a young girl.

> Telluride was a wide open town, saloons, gambling, and red-light districts with it's (sic) fancy girls and dance halls as fine as any you see on television or in a western movie. There was the Gold Belt, the Silver Bell, Big and Little Pick and Gad, Big and Little Sweden, maybe more. Just because we were little kids don't think we didn't have ears and eyes.

> (She and friends would pick wild flowers.) We'd pick bouquets of them and sell them to the ladies living on East Pacific Avenue. Besides the big dance halls there were rows of little houses. We'd knock on the doors, hold out the flowers and say 25 cents, and usually got it. We never went in any place, but weren't really afraid either, because we'd see the girls up town at the Post Office, or shopping, or just on the street. We knew them every time. No one else used powder, painted, had such red lips, fancy clothes, and hair-dos.

Ernest Hoffman recollected the red light district of his town as well. He was a young man living in Silverton after the turn-of-the century and remembered it with a somewhat romantic view:

> Books give a lot of those gals hell and maybe some of them deserve it, but there was a lot that have been pretty good. You take some of those guys up there—mining operators I'm talking about—some of the big shots that were up in Silverton during that time, you know, they married those women and, Jesus Christ, they made wonderful wives.

☦ *ix* ☧

You bet it was just like anybody else's business. They were in it for the money (They came from) all over; all over. Christ, they came from all over the world. I can remember when I was going to high school we had a couple of them from Hawaii. They called them the Honolulu Blondes.... No, they came from all over. They came from, hell, there was some of them, I know there was some Swedes and well, they were all nationalities and they catered to those guys, those miners.

When he was interviewed with author and mine manager, Allan Bird (*Bordellos of Blair Street*), Hoffman added:

As soon as they (miners) hit town they would head for Blair Street and blow all their money on gambling and women. . . . There were a lot of "do-gooders" in town that wanted to do away with the women, but Joe Terry and the other mine managers fought to keep them. It was important that the men remained in good spirits and the gambling and women served that purpose.

Max Evans' *Madame Millie* recounts the story of Mildred Cusey in her own language and through her experiences. A successful madam, she explained why some women turned to prostitution. She was working in Roswell, New Mexico at the time and learned to her surprise...

that Miss Emma (she ran a strict, almost proper whore house) had formerly been a schoolteacher who had been introduced to the business in the Indian Territory of Oklahoma. She and two other teachers had shared their tents with two prostitutes who couldn't find any other place to ply their trade. At that time, there weren't that many opportunities open for women in the West. Soon the two freelancers were making more money in a month than the three educators drew down in a whole year. They were duly impressed. When the whores decided to move to New Mexico, the teachers went along, representing their new friends at first, and all three branching out later in houses of their own.

Millie, like Nellie, was a strong personality and a good businesswoman. Their experiences were similar, although Millie, perhaps, can be said to have been the more successful and certainly had the more distinguished clientele. For both, it proved a rough life and a profession full of dangers and personal tribulations.

Even Mark Twain, writing about booming Virginia City, Nevada, in the early 1860s, commented about the girls. *Roughing It* describes the initial boom times of this famous silver district and town.

> Vice flourished luxuriantly during the heyday of our 'flush times.' The saloons were overburdened with customers; so were the police courts, the gambling dens, the brothels, and the jails—unfailing signs of high prosperity in a mining region—in any region for that matter. Is it not so? A crowded police-court docket is the surest of all signs that trade is brisk and money plenty.

Twain had observed one of the fanciest and most prosperous, and, one might be tempted to say "classic," red light districts in western and American history. Indeed, he was right that it signified flush times had arrived on the Comstock. He might have been bold enough to proclaim that Virginia City's district rivaled some of the best in the East, which eventually proved true. Huck Finn later observed: "Mr. Mark Twain, he told the truth mainly. There was things which he stretched, but mainly he told the truth." About Virginia City's district, he told the truth.

In the end, the red light district still fascinates people, just like it did young Ellen as she remembered it sixty years later, and Ernest Hoffman, or that youthful reporter Mark Twain. The sordid aspects blended into the past and rode off into the sunset, except for Millie, who experienced them first hand. Reality gave way to a romanticized memory of years of long ago. The legends and stories that remained failed to tell the real story of this aspect of Colorado's past. The San Juan mining region and its urban red light districts of the late nineteenth and early twentieth centuries will be the focus of this study, which tries to present the reality of this way of life. A more honest portrayal, hopefully, will create more understanding of a time and people.

Rush to the San Juans
Urbanization Arrives

As permanent settlement reached the isolated San Juans in the early 1870s, small mining camps emerged from the footsteps of the prospectors and miners. Some settlements would become towns—Silverton, Ouray, Lake City, Rico, Telluride, and eventually Creede. But most remained satellite camps of their larger neighbors. One latecomer, Durango, in its first year reached a population of nearly 2,400 and emerged as the region's smelter center and railroad hub.

All of the permanent towns had several things in common, including being the county seat, the major local business center, a transportation hub, possessing more social amenities, and boasting a larger population than any of their neighboring, smaller camps. They all proved to be survivors, as well. Each promised to be the "Eldorado of the San Juans," that place where gold and silver beckoned to those who had ambition and motivation.

Of all the Colorado settlement patterns, mining proved to be the most urbanized. In theory, miners had gold and silver to spend, yet no time to pioneer a total economic development or supporting settlement.

On their heels, however, quickly came those who saw potential profit. Businessmen and businesswomen developed the urbanization and services needed to support the miners working in the nearby hills and mountains. They were quickly joined by the denizens of the red light districts and others who completed the San Juaners' urban world.

Each one of these towns held in its economic orbit the nearby mining camps. For example, Silverton claimed Howardsville, Eureka, Animas Forks, Gladstone, Niegoldstown, Mineral Point and some others. However, Ouray had its eye on several of Silverton's northern camps, and, when the Red Mountain excitement opened in the 1880s, Ouray and Silverton fought each other like cats and dogs to bring the new district into its particular economic orbit. When Otto Mears built his Silverton Railroad into Red Mountain, the battle was over, and Silverton emerged victorious even though the vast majority of the mining district was in Ouray County.

Before there were any towns or camps, however, there were legends and rumors of rich mines and buried treasures. Spanish prospectors and miners had arrived back in the 1760s, prospecting the La Plata Mountains and pushing into the heart of the San Juans, certainly as far north as the future site of Silverton and beyond to Lake Como. Isolated far from the New Mexico settlements, and not willing to pay the Spanish King his "royal fifth" of all they found, these miners left behind few records of what they had unearthed or their mine locations. What they did leave behind, though, were those legends, rumors, and rich "lost" mine stories.

The California gold rush of 1848-49 gave birth to prospecting throughout the West, and the Pike's Peak Rush of 1859 did the same a decade later. So strong was the lure of gold that prospectors reached Baker's Park, where Silverton one day would be located, in 1860. At a day and time when anything and everything seemed possible, that feat led to a mining fiasco the next year. Discoverer Charles Baker promoted the isolated and elevated district as the "New Eldorado," with placer, or free gold, in the streams just waiting for one and all. Baker knew that would, in all probability, bring on a mining rush, and a rush was precisely what transpired. Over-promoted from the start, it proved a miserable failure, especially against the outbreak of the Civil War back East in the "States."

For almost the rest of the decade, the San Juans remained the quiet dominion of the Utes, who had lived around the edges of the mountains for centuries. That would not last, however. Back came the prospectors in 1869 and 1870, and again the San Juans beckoned as the New Eldorado. Tragedy followed, as the Utes stood in the way of the onrushing whites. Pressure built; the "Utes Must Go" became the rallying cry. By the end of 1873, they ceded the San Juans, although the Ute reservation still hemmed in the miners in every direction but to the east. By 1881, the Utes were gone, moved to Utah following the uproar over the murder of one of their agents Nathan Meeker. Only the Southern Utes remained well to the south along the New Mexico border, far away from mountains and the mining districts.

There might have been scoffers, but this time gold and silver prospects had been found in isolated southwestern Colorado. The minerals were there, but it would take some determination and courage to reach the new bonanza. The towering, rugged San Juan Mountains presented problems seldom confronted by the oncoming prospectors and miners earlier. Two writers of the era, Frank Fossett and Hubert Howe Bancroft, tried to describe the situation to their readers. Fossett wrote in the late 1870s:

> West of San Luis Park is one mass of mountains, thrown together in the most chaotic confusion. . . . The rugged and almost impassable character of the mountains and their vast extent and the heavy snows and long winters, have acted as serious drawbacks to growth and development. There is probably more country standing on edge in this section than anywhere else beneath the sun.

Bancroft's writings proved even more dramatic:

> It is the wildest and most inaccessible region in Colorado, if not in North America.... It is as if the great spinal column of the continent had bent upon itself in some spasm of the earth, until the vertebra overlapped each other, the effect being unparalleled ruggedness, and sublimity more awful than beautiful. Into this world would wander the hopeful, the desperate, and others, all dreaming of finding their fortune.

The San Juans challenged prospectors and miners with its elevation—the highest mining district in the United States and one of the world's most elevated. Some thought this a blessing because it was rumored that the higher the silver mine, the richer the ore. Hence, prospectors scurried around at 13,000 and 14,000 feet, searching for promising mineral outcroppings. Winter weather played a significant role as well, in a variety of ways, from transportation to quality of life. As one miner observed, when he tramped out of the San Juans, it was a place of "three months of mighty late fall, and nine months of damned hard winter."

That the rugged terrain and climate were serious obstacles could not be denied, but on came the adventuresome. By 1872, prospectors began to "pour" into the San Juans and, following the typical pattern, soon organized mining districts. No Colorado mining region proved more rugged, remote, elevated, or inaccessible, but that did not squelch the expectations of the excited fortune seekers of finding their bonanza.

Nor did such difficulties prevent the establishment of permanent settlements and the development of a transportation network. The easiest route to the San Juan mining district was from the south, up the Animas Valley into the Animas River Canyon, then through the mountains; however, that way also represented the most time consuming route, frustrating to the oncoming hopeful, as they raced to stake their claims.

Other possible routes took the eager prospectors over 12,000-13,000 foot mountain passes—Engineer, Cinnamon, and Stoney—no mean feat in the summer and usually impossible in the winter. It would take a while before a toll road snaked up the Uncompahgre Canyon and tied Ouray to its neighbors.

Eventually, that savior of the day, the railroad, arrived. The Denver & Rio Grande gave birth to the town of Durango and reached Silverton in 1882. The fortunate Silverton community became a railroad hub, with three smaller lines (Silverton, Silverton Northern, and Silverton, Gladstone & Northernly) eventually reaching beyond it into the nearby mining centers at Red Mountain, Animas Forks and Gladstone. By the 1890s, Telluride, Rico, Ouray, Creede and Lake City had also gained rail connections. They were the fortunate ones. The late nineteenth century community without a railroad was poor indeed and likely not to prosper.

But the trials and tribulations of opening a new mining district seemed worth it, for, as the saying went, mining offered the way to "get rich without working." As one old timer confessed, however, "I never worked so hard in my life to get rich without working." For most of the San Juaners and their mining contemporaries, that proved their life's epitaph in the various western mining districts—working hard without finding their long-sought bonanza.

The San Juans eventually confirmed expectations of being a mineral treasure box. Before the mining era ebbed, gold, silver, lead, zinc, copper, molybdenum, coal, and other valuable minerals would be found in or around the mountains. Even on its borders, pitchblende and carnotite were discovered, from which uranium would be refined. The first epic, though, belonged to silver. However, over-production and a small market for silver (beyond coins and jewelry) combined to produce a corresponding price decline and led to trouble for silver miners. When silver's era declined, gold seized the stage in the 1890s and held it for several decades. That era finally drew to a close as World War I seized the world's attention, but the San Juans had evolved into one of the major mining districts in American history. The dreams of the prospectors of the 1870s had been realized, if not always to their own personal satisfaction or benefit.

Meanwhile, the land encompassed by the San Juans had whirled through a series of county births and rebirths. Initially it had been in two counties, Lake and Conejos. Following the 1873 Ute cession, the next year saw the territorial legislature carve La Plata, Hinsdale, and Rio Grande counties out of the original two.

Then, in 1876, new San Juan County took the western part of Hinsdale, only to lose most of its territory the next year to newly-fashioned Ouray County. San Juan County thus became the only Western Slope county to retain exactly the same boundaries as it has today. Rio Grande joined the mix in 1879. Two years later Dolores arrived, and finally Mineral, thanks to the Creede excitement in the 1890s. These divisions reflected the current mining development and completed the process of counties dividing and birthing. The lure of mining had done it all.

It was against this background, then, that urbanization occurred in the San Juans. Mining could not exist without its partner. William Byers and his *Rocky Mountain News* (May 18, 1872) correctly predicated what would occur:

> All will be bustle, hurry, noise excitement and confusion. Doubtless there will be stores and saloons—the latter abounding—and these will be crowded with men whose pockets will be filled with big specimens, small silver bars, and rolls of location notices and assay certificates. Who can question the certainty that there will be enacted in that locality the same scenes of lawlessness which have traditionally attended such excitements, and that dance–houses will be filled with half or wholly tipsy miners, with, perhaps, a sprinkling of abandoned women.

Once it seemed assured that minerals existed in paying quantities, the familiar urban pattern emerged and mining communities took root. Each of the larger towns and the smaller camps followed this general model, but with some individual characteristics of their own.

Lake City gained early fame as the gateway to the San Juans. Located on the district's eastern flank, it offered relatively easy access to the western mining areas over elevated Cinnamon and Engineer passes. Its merchants also could tap the agricultural regions in the San Luis Valley, and the town's location further provided easier travel to Colorado's eastern slope. Unfortunately, the site had earlier gained some unwanted notoriety when Alferd Packer devoured some of his dead companions after they became snowbound during the winter of 1873-74.

By the mid-1870s, a settlement had taken hold along the Lake Fork of the Gunnison River. By the spring of 1875, with its thirteen log cabins, Lake City was launched into history. It also gained what every mining community needed to have, a newspaper, to promote, defend, and extol its virtues. And that is what the very first issue of the *Silver World,* in June 1876, did, with enthusiasm.

Lake City served not only as a gateway to the mountains but also as the business district for the mines on the eastern side of the San Juans. By July 8, 1876, the *Silver World* proudly reported that among the community's businesses were three assayers, two groceries, two assay offices, two boot and shoemakers, and one each of a cigar store, restaurant, blacksmith, billiard hall, meat market, drug store, hotel, and bakery. Not to mention, there also had arrived nine attorneys (new mining districts often became infamous for law suits) and three doctors. Somehow, the editor must have overlooked saloons, for they certainly existed in the town. Such rapid urban development proved typical for the mining West, as did the fact that saloons usually outnumbered other businesses.

Stage routes connected Lake City with Saguache and Del Norte and, eventually, to Silverton and Ouray. The 1870s proved to be the best days for Lake City. Unfortunately, its tributary mines never equaled the best of those farther west, and, in November 1879, that curse of mining communities, fire, "inflicted a severe blow upon (its) present growth and

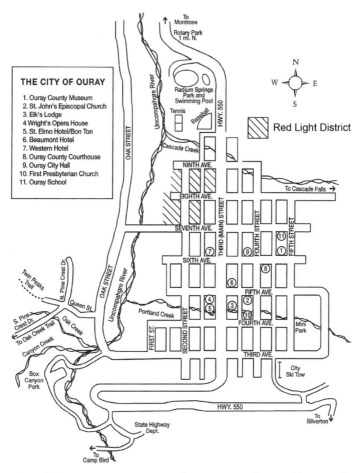

THE CITY OF OURAY

1. Ouray County Museum
2. St. John's Episcopal Church
3. Elk's Lodge
4 Wright's Opera House
5. St. Elmo Hotel/Bon Ton
6. Beaumont Hotel
7. Western Hotel
8. Ouray County Courthouse
9. Ouray City Hall
10. First Presbyterian Church
11. Ouray School

Red Light District

prosperity." Of the San Juan towns, Lake City was the smallest, and its premier mining days, the shortest. Not even the arrival of the Denver & Rio Grande in 1889 revived its fortunes.

In contrast, Silverton would be able to claim a century of mining days. Located in Baker's Park, along the banks of the Animas River, the site had gained a bit of notoriety thanks to the Baker fiasco of 1861-62. Now it proved a perfect location for a community. When the prospectors returned in the 1870s, the park became a natural headquarters before moving beyond, into the heart of the San Juans. Byers, in his *News,* however, warned his readers about another San Juan "humbug." It would take awhile before Colorado's leading newspaperman would finally concede that this growing excitement was not another daydream.

As a result of mining, settlement came to the valley. Two little camps quickly emerged—Howardsville, at the western end of the trail over Stony Pass and down Cunningham Gulch, and Silverton, down the valley a couple of miles to the south, nestled along the Animas River between Cement and Mineral Creeks. Incorporated in November 1876, Silverton reportedly had two general stores, five saloons, two hotels, drug store, bakery, butcher, grocery store, and four lawyers that spring.

The two settlements quickly became rivals, particularly over which would be the county seat, an all-important designation. That designation equated with prosperity and prominence for the town that gained the prize. It meant folks coming to town for a variety of reasons, a foundation for permanence, and political standing worth fighting for in a winner-take-all contest.

Initially, Howardsville won when the territorial legislature gave it the prize. Silverton, however, would not easily concede the honor and forced a county election. That finally resolved the dispute, with Silverton winning handily; not to mention that it also gained a smelter and a sawmill along the way, both essential to the town's future. Unwilling to leave any stone unturned, Silvertonians launched a road building campaign to the south, down the Animas Valley, where ranchers and farmers had already settled, hoping to tap the Silverton trade and the San Juan mining market in general. That further strengthened its position as did the coming of the railroad.

Meanwhile, Howardsville peaked and declined. Such proved to be the fate of the loser in such an all important struggle. Nor was Silverton finished bolstering its position in the San Juans.

When the railroad finally arrived, in July 1882, Silverton's isolation ended. Almost immediately mineral production increased in the district dramatically and the community was on its way to becoming one of Colorado's premier mining towns. Eventually, it became the railroad hub of the San Juans, with four lines meeting there.

Over the mountains, Ouray emerged a formidable rival, with one major advantage—easy access along the Uncompahgre River to the farming and ranching lands beyond. Founded in the mid-seventies like Silverton, at Ouray's doorstep sat the Ute Reservation, hemming the community in from the north. Not until the Utes left the region would the town and its mines reach their full potential, helped along by the arrival of the Denver & Rio Grande Railroad in 1887.

Ouray had other advantages—a beautiful location combined with ease of access, plus those medical wonders of the nineteenth century, hot springs, which rapidly made the town a tourist mecca. Ouray soon got into a fight with Silverton over which was the gateway to the "bonanza" Red Mountain Mining District. Yet even with the help of that toll road-building entrepreneur, Otto Mears, Ouray could not overcome Silverton's early railroad connections. Mears played a role in both communities, as he built transportation outlets to each. However, his Silverton Railroad to Red Mountain and Ironton gave Silverton the dominate position.

Ouray's sparring with Silverton over those promising mines reflected the typical nineteenth century urban jealousy. Rico became jealous of Silverton, Silverton jealous of Ouray, Ouray jealous of Lake City, and vise versa, particularly in the early years of mining in the San Juans. Durango and Telluride would later join the fray. The competition sometimes became editorially hot, such as when Lake City's *Silver World* (May 13, 1876) called Ouray an "unmitigated fraud and humbug."

Let some outsider dare criticize the region and its mines and/or communities, though, and the defensive editorials arose unanimously from these erstwhile rivals to defend their "turf" against any and all outsiders. Again, to quote the *Silver World* (October 13, 1875), when such criticism appeared, "We rejoice at their (neighboring towns) prosperity as in our own. Each adds its portion of development to the great San Juan country."

Rico was the third of the major San Juan mining towns to appear on the scene. Located on the western edge of the region, along the Dolores River, it was even more isolated than Ouray and Silverton. Miners coming out of Arizona had prospected the area in 1869, but it would be a decade before permanent settlement arrived.

By August 1879, six blocks of the town had been surveyed and subdivided into lots. Similar to what happened elsewhere, a disagreement arose over what to name the community. "Rico" won over Carbonate City, Dolores City, Carbonateville, Lead City, and Doloresville. The December 5th municipal election created a city government, and Rico marched into its future.

Meanwhile, the editor of the *Dolores News,* September 23, 1879, quickly explained to his readers what his paper meant to Rico, "A mining camp without a newspaper is indeed a flat and insipid place. A live newspaper in a mining camp is worth to it millions of dollars." How would this happen? "The outside world can have but little knowledge of its existence and the owners of its mines have no hope but to remain in a state of masterly inactivity," without a journalistic spokesman. To bring this point home, he concluded, "The day a camp begins to show signs of being unable to sustain a newspaper, no surer indication of decay could possibly be found."

That being true, and without question it certainly was, then Telluride could count on a wonderful future. Over the first decade of its existence, six newspapers, at one time or another, promoted its wonders. During Telluride's peak mineral production and population, in the 1890s and early 1900s, local readers had a choice of four newspapers. If nothing else, however, these totals go to show how transitory and perilous the life of a mining community newspaper could be.

The other fact shown was that Telluride had emerged as the largest and wealthiest of the San Juan mining towns. During its greatest years, which ended in 1923, the local mines produced over $90,000,000 in silver and gold, compared with runners-up Ouray ($67,000,000) and Silverton ($42,000,000). Add to this, the copper, lead, and zinc mined, and the significance of the San Juan mines appears. The reader should keep in mind that prices for minerals were much lower then. For example, gold was $20 and change per ounce and silver slipped steadily down from $1.35 to under $1 an ounce.

First named "Columbia" when founded in 1878, the settlement changed its name to "Telluride" (after the ore) in 1883. Development proved slow because of its isolation on the western end of the San Juans. Finally, the railroad chugged into town in 1890, and completed a route from Durango to Ridgway the next year. With its isolation resolved for most of the year, Telluride's great mining era opened. The 1899 *Colorado Mining Directory* illustrated this point. It listed, among other businesses, two banks, six grocery stores, two hotels, six restaurants, two shoe stores, three assayers, and twenty-two saloons, along with twelve lawyers and an undertaker.

While Telluride grew slowly, Creede literally exploded on the scene in the early 1890s. If any San Juan camp lived up to the "wild and woolly" image of the public's imagination, Creede embodied expectations. As its newspaperman, Cy Warman, sang, "It is day all day in the daytime and there is no night in Creede." When that "dirty little coward (Bob Ford)," the man who killed Jesse James, was himself killed there, it only enhanced the image. And then legendary con man, Soapy Smith, seemingly gained control of the red light district and briefly ran the town. Creede's fame, or infamy, spread even further abroad.

During the 1891-92 rush, Creede's cost of living soared, not an unusual occurrence for a young mining community. Nor did the cost come down much, even after the railroad reached the town in late 1891 (the D&RG had only been a dozen or so miles away when the rush started). As one shocked visitor exclaimed, whiskey "that does not kill cannot be had for less than 25 cents per glass." The new *Creede Candle,* January 7, 1892, thought otherwise, however, and reported "from first to last" town development "is guided by as enterprising and rustling class of merchants and business men that ever got together to build a city."

Creede's day lasted all too briefly. As mentioned, the over-production of silver, plus the declining world-wide use of it in coinage, steadily led to a decline in the metal's price. Federal government support, by coining silver dollars, did not help. With the crash and depression of 1893, and the end of Uncle Sam's silver purchasing, silver's era and Creede's boom ended. Production would continue into the new century, but the spark went out in the declining mining community.

Throughout all of this, one San Juan community had grown steadily and later emerged the largest town on Colorado's Western Slope. The child of the Denver & Rio Grande, Durango had opened in 1880. The next year, the trains arrived, and, before all was said and done, Durango had railroads stretching in all four directions, including the Rio Grande Southern and the Denver & Rio Grande.

While the nearest productive mineral mines lay fifteen miles west in the La Plata Mountains, Durango eventually became the regional smelter center for the San Juans because of its lower elevation. It also had the region's only productive coal mines in close proximity. To add to its attractions, Durango contained the largest business district, a much more temperate climate, and nearby agricultural land, containing increasing numbers of ranches and farms. Never missing an opportunity to grow, Durangoans pushed to have the neighboring Ute Reservation opened for settlement, and they succeeded in 1899. Add to this, nearby tourist attractions—Mesa Verde, the Southern Utes, hot springs, and, after the railroad arrived, the easiest access into the mountains and the world beyond the Animas Valley—and Durango's future looked promising indeed.

Durangoans matched that future, and, by the century's turn, its population of 3,317 justified the expectations of its founders. Although never a mining community, as were the other towns, its growth during its first two decades depended heavily on the mines to the north in the San Juans. Silverton, Rico, and even Telluride to an extent, equally depended on Durango's smelter to refine their ores.

The "big six" had the publicity, developments, and mines to justify the huge share of the press coverage they received. At the same time, though, over three dozen smaller camps flourished for a season or two—and sometimes a decade or longer—and all of them offered temptations in their red light districts. As for those smaller settlements, a couple of girls might have shown up in the summer to constitute a seasonal "attraction" in the camps. During the summer season, miners found it easier to mine and ship ore, and the camps' populations took a brief upward swing. Once fall appeared, the girls departed along with many of their customers, for the more inviting and profitable towns.

This, then, was the world of the San Juan prostitutes, a world that Nellie would join as the mining districts and towns entered into their decline. Only Durango would continue to grow, albeit slowly, as its economy turned more to agriculture and tourism. The wide-open days faded, along with the mines, camps, and towns; but they left behind a legend, a legend that would prove profitable in days to come.

Population of San Juan Towns

For some reason, only one of the San Juan mining towns was reported in the Federal census count in 1880. Durango, of course, was not in existence, nor was Creede.

State Census

	1876(est.)	1880	1885	1890	1900	1910
Silverton	600		1,195	1,154	1,360	2,153
Telluride			561	839	2,446	1,756
Rico		891	571	1,134	811	368
Ouray	250		1,103	2,534	2,196	1,644
Lake City	700		783	607	700	405
Creede					938	741
Durango			2,254	2,726	3,317	4,686

City Revenue Source or Sinful Pleasure?

As may be imagined, the city fathers in the San Juan towns wrestled with the question of the red light district. Not only did this obviously include prostitution; but gambling, drinking, and low class theaters also caught their attention. No "real" mining community could afford to be without the profitable enterprise of prostitution or its sister vices. Heaven forbid, customers might go elsewhere if they were not available. Yet at the same time, the "vice" district definitely violated Victorian moral standards and the era's idealized concepts of women and wives, mothers, and homemakers.

In the end, the towns reached their angle of repose and allowed the red light districts to remain, although each district had to be as much out of sight as possible. To reach this point, a whole series of ordinances were set in place.

Complaints came early about the "ungodly business." Silverton "citizens," in May 1877, asked their city board "to restrict dance houses and houses of that class" to within certain "limits and bounds." They asked for a special meeting, which they achieved two days later on

May 21. Next, they presented their petition, "praying the board to restrict dance houses within certain limits." Forty-eight residents signed the petition. Then came a second petition signed by eighty, "praying the board to either suppress entirely, the above mentioned houses or to take no notice of them." After discussion, the board accepted the first petition as an ordinance to be drafted. Then it defeated the second and promptly adjourned. Silverton did not get around to writing an ordinance regarding prostitution until April 1881, which then went into effect the next month. The ordinance made it:

> Unlawful to keep a bawdy house, house of ill-fame, or knowingly permit any house to be used for the same within the city limits, or within three miles of same.
> $25-300 fine

> Unlawful to be an inmate of such a house or commit acts of prostitution.
> $10-100 fine

> Unlawful to employ lewd women, or women, having a reputation as a prostitute, as a carrier of beer or any other articles, drink, or to sing, or dance in lewd or indecent manner or permit any women as bartender in any such place or frequent any such house, shop, or saloon.
> $10-100 fine

> Unlawful for any person or persons to keep a house or place where lewd or disorderly, persons, or women, with a reputation as a prostitute to assemble for dancing or singing within the town or within three miles.
> $25-300 fine

Unlawful to appear in a state of nudity or dress not belonging to his or her sex or an indecent or lewd dress or make an indecent exposure.
$10-100 fine

(Silverton Ordinance Book A, 1879. *Ordinances of the Town of Silverton* Silverton: Board of Trustees, 1905)

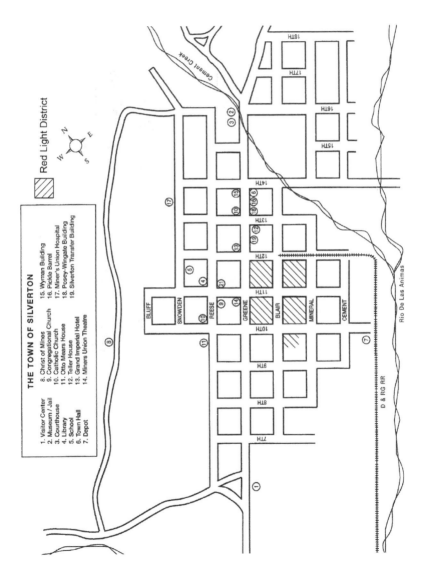

That seemed to have covered all possibilities, or so Silvertonians hoped, and so did all the other communities who passed similar ordinances to regulate sin. The problem for all—"Do we really want this enforced?"

Lake City's indecision concerning the prostitution question illustrated the problems the city fathers faced. They thought they covered all possible bases with their ordinance in February, 1881. "No bawdy house, house of ill fame, house of assignation, disorderly house of any description whatever and house or place for promiscuous dance after the usual manner of a dance house" would be allowed. Furthermore, "no house or place for dancing or other amusement injurious to the morals of the town and its inhabitants" would be allowed. For such misbehavior, a fine of $100 to $300 awaited the transgressors as well as the possibility of imprisonment for not less than "thirty days nor more than 90 days."

Not completely satisfied with that action, the board passed an October 1884 ordinance stating that none of the above would be allowed to operate within the Lake City limits, except in the specified area—"south of town and west of Bluff St." Four years later, the council repealed that law and passed a new ordinance stating that "no bawdy house, dance house" will be allowed within the corporate city limits, with the same set of fines as in 1881. Then, in January of 1893, the bawdy houses, dance houses, and so forth were not allowed within the city or, within "three miles" of the city limits, but the fine was dropped to $5-100.

The city fathers also tackled the issue of minors in and around the red light district. That emotional issue proved one of the "hot" topics of the day that swirled around town. Initially, the *Silver World* (January 15, 1876) reported the city had decided that upon "the complaint of a parent or guardian" it would investigate such complaints. A person allowing a youth "under twelve in a billiard or 'ball' alley" had to pay the town a fine of $25. Then, an 1881 ordinance declared, "no person under twelve years of age" may "play or frequent billiards halls, bowling alleys, shooting galleries," and the law included a number of other no-no's. In 1884, that was broadened to cover another potential tempting situation, "no minor may assist in a dance hall or remain for any purpose in a bawdy house or dance hall" (*Lake City Ordinance Book, February 1881-1914*).

The question as to what age a youth would be allowed in the district varied. Lake City might have set the age at twelve, Silverton put the age at eighteen, and Durango pushed it to twenty-one. A fine not exceeding $100 awaited anyone in Durango who allowed any under age person "to loiter, stroll about or frequent such a place," unless the youngster "is accompanied by parent or guardian."

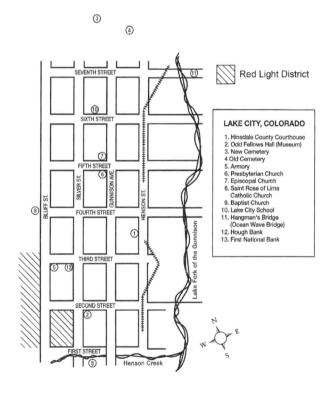

Rico's prostitution ordinance proved similar to its two San Juan neighbors. However, opium caught the board of trustees' attention and resulted in the following 1890 ordinance:

It shall be unlawful for any person or persons to maintain or keep any house or resort where smoking or other unnatural use of opium or any compound there of is practiced.

Any person upon conviction thereof shall be fined no less than 25 dollars or more than 50 dollars, and it shall be unlawful for any person to frequent or visit such resort for the purpose of indulging in the use of opium or any other compound thereof.

Any such person or persons found in such a house or resort shall be fined not less than $5 nor more than $10. (*Rico Book of Ordinances I, 1880-1881*)

Failure to observe closing on the Sabbath brought forth another Rico Ordinance:

If any person shall be guilty of open lewdness or other notorious acts of public indecency, tending to debauch the public morals, or shall keep open any tippling or gaming house on the Sabbath day or night … to the encouragement of idleness, gaming, drinking, fornication or other misbehavior, within the corporate limits of the Town of Rico, or within one mile beyond, every such person shall, on conviction, be fined not less than $2 nor more than $100 or imprisoned in the town jail not exceeding 90 days, or by both such fine and imprisonment at the discretion of the court.

Like their neighbors, Ricoites worried about minors frequenting saloons. The board decided that a "notice must be posted in each and every saloon. By resolution of the Board of Trustees of the Town of Rico—No minor allowed here—a violation of this Resolution will cause the license to be revoked."

Temple of Music, Ouray
Parlor Room, Ouray Red Light District
Courtesy Ouray County Historical Society

Ouray followed suit with an 1883 ordinance covering gambling and bawdy houses. That ordinance included several different features:

> It shall be lawful for the marshal and police officers in executing the duties to break open doors for the purpose of taking possession of gambling devices and all persons having such gambling devices may without complaint or warrant be conveyed before some justice of the peace to be dealt with according to the law.

> If an owner refuses to allow an officer in lawful manner to enter by force and to arrest without warrant all suspicious persons found there in (sic), the obstructing

person shall be deemed guilty of a misdemeanor. $25-300 fine.

In the spring of 1883, a Ouray resident became upset over such activities and asked the city fathers to take some step "in regard to the social evil now existing promiscuously throughout the town." The March request was duly filed, but apparently nothing resulted from the complaint. This led to a May 9 complaint about a dance hall. Strangely, the end result produced an ordinance "regulating and licensing show, exhibitions and amusement," with nary a mention of red light district activities. (*Ouray Book No. 5* containing the minutes of the proceedings of the Board of Trustees of the town of Ouray, January 1, 1882 to June 16, 1888)

The settlement of Columbia, which eventually evolved into Telluride, faced some of the same problems as its neighbors. Sometimes folks on both sides of an issue circulated petitions. Such occurred in May of 1882, when residents pleaded for removing "all dance halls from Colorado Avenue." Their opponents countered with a petition against "said removal." The council promptly laid both petitions on the table and moved to have an ordinance concerning dance halls written, which was read and quickly passed in June.

Telluride carefully defined where the red light district could exist to prevent its activities from intruding elsewhere. The marshal was instructed "to enforce strictly the ordinances against prostitution outside of the territory." If any prostitute conducted business outside of the specified territory, a fine was in order.

Columbia also worried about law officers gambling and declared at a January 8, 1883 meeting that if a marshal was found gambling "his office would be declared vacant." Furthermore, "any man or woman who lives together in an open state of adultery or fornication or both" caught Telluride's notice. The fine could not exceed $300. And also, "the offense will be sufficiently proved by circumstances which shall raise presumption of co-habitation and unlawful intimacy." "Nudity and indecent exposure" captured the council's attention as well, as did

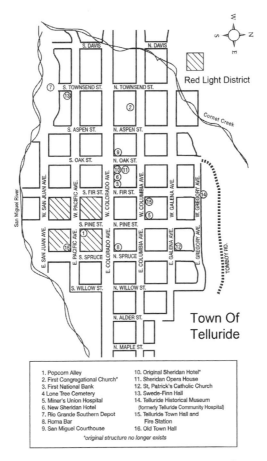

Red Light District

Cornet Creek

San Miguel River

Town Of
Telluride

TOMBOY RD.

1. Popcorn Alley
2. First Congregational Church*
3. First National Bank
4. Lone Tree Cemetery
5. Miner's Union Hospital
6. New Sheridan Hotel
7. Rio Grande Southern Depot
8. Roma Bar
9. San Miguel Courthouse
10. Original Sheridan Hotel*
11. Sheridan Opera House
12. St. Patrick's Catholic Church
13. Swede-Finn Hall
14. Telluride Historical Museum
    (formerly Telluride Community Hospital)
15. Telluride Town Hall and
    Fire Station
16. Old Town Hall

*original structure no longer exists

"indecent or lewd books or pictures or exhibit or perform any indecent, immoral or lewd play." If convicted of such an offense, the guilty party, or parties, faced a fine that ranged from $25-300 (Minutes of the Board of Trustees Columbia, Book 1, June 5, 1880-April 10, 1883).

As the 1890s dawned, Creede arrived as the last major San Juan town on the scene and quickly gained a wide-open reputation. However that "epoch" proved of short duration because the crash of 1893 ended its boom and the presence of rambunctious youth. To keep control of the situation, the council hired a police force. The police commission oversaw the policemen and marshal and tried to carefully regulate the force. At their own expense, policemen had to purchase regulation uniforms and also a badge, after which they would receive the $75 per

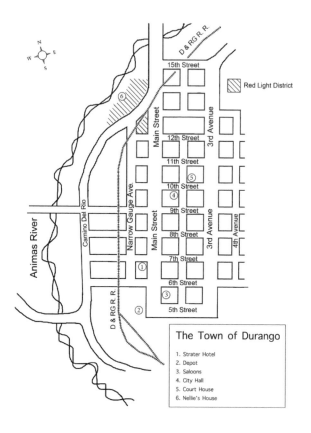

The Town of Durango

1. Strater Hotel
2. Depot
3. Saloons
4. City Hall
5. Court House
6. Nellie's House

month salary. The marshal was paid $100 per month and also had to "dress himself in a regulation policemen's uniform" at his own expense, and wear the badge of his office at all times. He was subject to the mayor's orders as well as the police commission's orders.

For daily risking one's life and enduring the stresses that came with the job, these were not particularly high compensations. However, even in boom days these wages ranked near the top of the salary scale and were much better than that received by miners and store clerks.

One of the officers' jobs was to arrest "any woman who shall frequent any saloon, tippling house or gambling house or who shall drink at the bar of such saloon or engage or participate in any games of chance or cards in such saloon, tippling house or gambling house." Even in wide-open Creede, such activities remained frowned upon by much of the general public.

Hard times hit Creede soon after its birth, as was previously mentioned. The economic crash and subsequent depression hung around for almost the rest of the decade, ending the hoped-for opportunity for years of local prosperity. The city council soon found itself strapped for money and requested its citizens' views on keeping the night marshal. The following responses tell much about what people thought about law and order versus expenses:

> Both should be retained, it is good protection especially in case of fire.
> Keep him and if any taken off, let it be the day marshal.
> We should have both.
> It don't (sic) make much difference to me.
> Take him off. I don't think it is any protection.
> Don't remove him, it is the cheapest protection we could have. (*Book 1, Minutes of City Council, July 18, 1892-November 1, 1908*)

A similar response might have come from any of the towns undergoing the financial crisis of the 1890s—or perhaps at any other time.

Durango, the railroad hub and smelter center, faced comparable problems as well and responded similarly to its counterparts in the mountains. Durangoans also were concerned about children and the temptations of the red light district. "Any boy or girl" found on the public streets after nine in the evening "without being accompanied by a parent or guardian," or not "able to give a good account of themselves" would be fined from $2-10. Although the parents most likely paid the fine, the penalty was levied on the child.

Boys and girls under age sixteen, out after nine, had better be able to give a "good account of themselves, himself or herself." A fine of, again, $2-10 awaited the convicted children that were, or they could be "imprisoned in the city jail for a period of not more than 10 days." That would have been quite an experience, if the penalty came to that point. Not stopping there, males twenty-one years of age and females eighteen years or younger "are not to be in or about saloons, billiards, gambling houses, houses of ill fame or any show or theater where obscene plays are performed." One exception existed—the "pursuit of some lawful business."

It is interesting to see the spread of ages (twelve to twenty-one) addressed by various towns' ordinances. Apparently, San Juaners could not decide what constituted the age of maturity for the young folk, but then again, neither could other Victorians elsewhere.

Telluride Parlor House 1975
Courtesy Duane A. Smith

"Fornication among unmarried adults" continued as a "less desired" activity! Apparently a bit more shocked than some of their neighbors, Durangoans conducted a much larger sweep to capture its practitioners. Such goings-on were not to be performed in "any room in any building or on any highway or other place within Durango." The guilty would be fined from $10-50. Once again, just the "presumption of cohabitation and unlawful intimacy" provided proof of such sinfulness.

For all this, the red light district continued to be a moneymaker for Durango's coffers. The records of October 1888 found $65 dollars collected, although a year later, in September, the amount slipped to $45. Silverton, on the other hand, had fifty-two prostitutes in May, 1904, who donated $260 to the city treasury.

Durango, like its neighbors, also wrestled with the opium "evil." One could not "keep, sell, barter or give it away." The seriousness of the offense was shown by a fine of $50 to $550. The fine for anyone using "opium or any preparations thereof" was also steep, $50 to $250. The ordinance did exclude druggists and persons who "sell opium as medicine." The last statement must have presented problems in separating the fraudulent from the honest. (*Durango Ordinance Book I, May 17, 1881 to June 6, 1888*)

Without a doubt, the law enforcement agents were kept busy in all the towns. Not only did they have the red light districts, as well as all the above issues, to check on to maintain law and order; but they also had a variety of other duties. These included the always present problems concerning the over-population of dogs, drunks, a variety of petty crimes, personal matters such as family abuse, and, in Ouray's case, ensuring that no Sunday baseball games desecrated the Sabbath with such frivolity.

The red light district contributed to the town's treasury in other ways. Licenses for acceptable businesses versus the district's businesses showed a marked disparity in the fee's charged, rather akin to a Victorian sin tax. Durango, for example, charged theaters, dance houses, and variety shows, respectively, $500, $300 and $200 per year, with a fine of $100-

300 for failure to obtain one. Liquor licenses displayed the same pattern at $400 per year. Upset owners of these businesses promptly protested these rates with little success, at least initially.

Contrast these with "acceptable" business fees. Durango charged, for example, the following—second hand stores, $25; livery stable, $10; insurance companies, $5 for each agent; and express wagons, $15.

Telluride's license fees proved similar in trend. Dance halls had to post a bond of $500 and observe the local ordinances. When they opened for business, they had to purchase a license for another $25 per year. Stepping out of line might mean forfeiting both sums, or losing the license. Hotels, restaurants, and boarding houses paid only $5, as did lodging houses, merchants, and laundries.

As an outcast and a necessity, as a town attraction and town detraction, the red light district flourished during the heyday of the San Juan mining district. Condemned from the pulpit but hailed as a business necessity, it survived. A community revenue source and at the same time a drain on the city budget, the district was viewed by many residents and visitors alike, as a sure sign of a "real" mining community, one that prospered and flourished in the best of times. When the girls, the gamblers, and their cohorts left, it was a hard-to-ignore indication that the beginning-of-the-end had come for the high times and prosperity.

Despite the crime, the cost to the city, the medical problems, and the social concerns, these were the reasons that the district was allowed to stay. Certainly, if at all possible, the district was placed in a very discrete location. The city fathers usually regulated by city ordinance so that proper folk would not be offended by seeing the sights and hearing the sounds or meeting the girls and pimps on the street. Nor did they want the Red Light denizens waltzing through local neighborhoods. That would be offensive to respectable women and might tempt youngsters to ask embarrassing questions. Yet as mentioned at the start of this chapter, the community did not want to lose the miners and mining business because of an upswing in civic virtue.

In the end, necessity, profits, and reality triumphed over image, reform, and virtue. Ordinances were passed and laws established, but did they really curtail the red light district? Not at first. It flourished, as will be seen in the next two chapters, and the district provided revenue and entertainment that overcame the arguments of those who questioned the necessity of the district.

Reformers and concerned folks might shake their heads, but the current of the times was going against them. They would eventually win, but not so much for what they said or managed to accomplish. That must have been small consolation for those who stood foursquare against such sin and vice.

They won, yet it might have been a pyrrhic victory because it was brought about more by the local economic situation, than by a moral uplifting of the community and its now declining number of residents. However, by the time their grandchildren and great-grandchildren arrived to visit the mining town where their ancestors once resided, the "Red Light District" had usually become legendary and a part of a past that rapidly had taken on a romantic glow. Money had been the name of the game in the red light district, and tourist dollars were still the name of the game in the modern San Juan communities that were not shy about profiting from their "sinful" past.

1. *Silverton Ordinance Book A, 1879*. Ordinances of the Town of Silverton (Silverton: Board of Trustees, 1905).

2. *Lake City Ordinance Book, February 1881-1914*.

3. *Rico Book of Ordinances I, 1880-1881*.

4. *Ouray Book No. 5* containing the minutes of the proceedings of the Board of Trustees of the town of Ouray, January 1, 1882 to June 16, 1888.

5. *Minutes of Board of Trustees Columbia, Book 1, June 5, 1880-April 10, 1883.*

6. *Book 1, Minutes of City Council, July 18,1892-November 1, 1908.*

7. *Durango Ordinance Book I, May 17, 1881-December 4, 1900.*

Working the Line
Prostitution in the San Juans,
1870s-1890s

The ordinances had been written, passed, and now had become part of city statutes. The question lingers, however, did these actions make any difference? What impact did government regulations have on the red light district, the prostitutes, and their pimps?

The "fair but frail" arrived with urbanization of the San Juans and became as much of its history as the legendary prospector and his burro. That one-time Nevada miner, Mark Twain, writing his wife Olivia, had this to say about them with a sideswipe at missionaries: "Infatuation for a filthy prostitute can make a man rival the Jesuit missionaries at their grandest and finest." Many of his mining contemporaries did not agree with him. The prostitute, or by whatever *non de plum* one chooses to call her, was one of the pioneers of the San Juan and Colorado, as she was throughout the mining West.

Most San Juan and Colorado camps and towns chose to accept and ignore prostitution, with one notable exception, Leadville. That booming town, in its heyday, boastfully compared its red light district with the best tenderloin districts in the nation. The more sedate or dignified San Juan communities generally only mentioned the district and girls if something criminal occurred, citizens' complaints arose, or a death of one of those "gone wrong" occurred.

Two realities certainly led to the eventual appearance of the district and its line. First, and perhaps foremost, was a shortage of women. Typical of the early days of a mining region, this led to the "need" for the "erring sisters." Both Lake City's *Silver World* (July 24, 1875) and Rico's *Dolores News* (September 23, 1879) contained stories about the need for "female emigration of the virtuous and industrious class." The editors estimated that the ratio of men to women was near "100 to 1." Some men tired of "the isolation of a miner's life" and put notices in the newspaper that they were "desiring correspondence with a limited number of young ladies."

Second, San Juaners displayed a greater tolerance of the district than would have been found in a similar sized Midwestern or Eastern village. The Rev. George Darley, a pioneering Presbyterian minister in Lake City in the mid-1870s had this to say about officiating at a funeral for Magg Hartman, who lived in "Hell's Acre":

> If the whole human race were constituted alike—all of the same temperament, all having equal advantages— then we might be able to judge all correctly; but, since there are such differences, we should be very slow in passing harsh judgment on anyone…
>
> I trust that all Christians, while they cannot reasonably be expected to feel as kindly toward the fallen as some do, will remember that –
> There's no life so lone and low
> But strength may yet be given,
> From narrowest lot on earth to grow
> The straighter up to Heaven.

Darley befriended his "peculiar friends" but broke his health, as he "suffered and suffered again," taking his ministry throughout the region. Those he ministered to appreciated his attitude and efforts and responded.

> Mr. Darley, there is one hundred and thirty-seven dollars from the boys; not one cent is from a church member. You have given us hell for five years; but you have always given it to us in the teeth. You have been kind to us when we were sick, and never said one word against the dead. We are sorry you are going away and this is to show our appreciation.

As the mines and communities opened in the 1870s, little mention of the red light districts graced the pages of local newspapers. Perhaps the editors wished to place their individual community's respectable face forward to entice potential investors, settlers, and visitors. They certainly desired, in general, to present their respectable Victorian faces to the world. The prevailing attitudes of their eastern cousins, regarding prostitution or sex, were good enough for them. So, at least for a while, San Juan newspapers avoided nearly all matters of a sexual nature.

When times change, so do attitudes. As the 1880s opened and moved forward, an evolution in attitude occurred. The editors and their communities may have felt a little more secure, a bit more willing to talk about all aspects of their life and times. As the editor of the *Dolores News* (March 18, 1882) explained, with perhaps tongue in cheek, "Prostitution creates less consternation than troublesome respectability." No doubt he had readers agreeing with him.

There also existed another factor. Prostitution was considered a positive sign of a prosperous, booming mining camp or town. After all, one had only to look at Leadville and its claim that its red light district rivaled the best in New York City (supposedly number one in the nation). Aspen, with a number of erring sisters who flocked there and its increased mining production in the late 1880s, threatened Leadville's claim as Colorado's number one mining district and town. No matter what the rank, established mining communities had to "promote" their "wayward" districts to be a "real" town and attract business.

Occasionally, the *Silverton Miner* would look at its local district with a bit of humor. A September 3, 1881 story featured Maggie Rothschild, a "Blair St. Belle." According to the report, she "went out calling attired in a unique costume." It consisted "of a pair of slippers and a gold chain." That proved too much for the night watchman who "escorted her to the town calaboose." Generally such goings on were discreetly left off the local news column.

One thing transpired, showing that prostitution had seasonal highs and lows for both camps and town. When summer came the girls arrived, when snow threatened they departed isolated camps and even towns. Silverton's *La Plata Miner,* in its September 10, 1881 issue, noted that the "notorious prostitute and thief Bronco Lou" had been lynched in New Mexico. Lou had been a summer visitor to the town and "proprietress of a dance house."

Newspapers also announced the arrivals of the girls, whether intentional or not, and gave them a bit of publicity. "Three female divines," noted the *Red Mountain Pilot* (March 10, 1883), now graced the community—"Long Annie of Silverton and Mollie Foley and Lizzie Gaylor of Durango (who) were among the arrivals this morning." For Red Mountain, just on the threshold of boom, this obviously represented a positive sign. For the ladies, it not only offered a chance of being the first on the scene, but the opportunity to get "settled" for the brief upcoming spring and summer seasons, which brought prospectors, investors, visitors, and miners to the mining district. Even in flush times, little Red Mountain never proved big enough to support a full-time line like its larger neighbors.

Neither was Animas Forks, over the mountain, east of Red Mountain. Despite its small size, it had its girls in season. The *Animas*

Belle McCoy
Courtesy of Duane A. Smith

Forks Pioneer, August 19, 1882 issue, announced that the stage leaving for a "lower attitude," in this case Silverton, departed with the soiled doves.

The editor of Telluride's *Evening Journal*, July 30, 1884, pointed to another "positive" sign, the arrival of the girls in a small camp nearby. "A herd of soiled doves will invade Ophir this week. It is the best sign of money being there." Portland received a similar greeting from neighboring Ouray's *Solid Muldoon* (August 2, 1889). The prostitutes there, "incline to Bacchanalian pleasures." Editor Dave Day thought though that perhaps a "round up of that village would fill the bill" for reform.

Meanwhile, over in Lake City, a resident who knew the girls explained why they worked in that occupation. Some of them stayed on the line "because that represented the kind of life they want to live," while others were "forced there by circumstances." In the latter class was one who, as a young orphan, had "heard about the good times at Lake City."

Expecting to find work there, she found none, and had "fallen prey to one of the so-called madams." She had never wanted to "be bad." The same individual also observed with a touch of Victorian sentimentality that "she is not the only girl there" who did not "want to be bad." As noted earlier, though, once in the profession, it proved hard to get out and "back to respectability." A reformed prostitute, however, provided positive testimony to the success of those trying to save the women from a "fate worse than death."

Speaking of Lake City, the census of 1880 disclosed some interesting facts about the local prostitutes. Belle, Mattie, Hattie, Ada, Millie, Gertrude, Mollie, and their friends were all between twenty and twenty-two, with only one exception, a girl who was twenty-four. Most came from the Midwest, except two from New York, and all were white and American-born. One was widowed and the rest single.

In 1885, Colorado did a state census. The returns from Ouray showed a similar pattern to Lake City's, five years earlier. The ages of the "sporting women" had a slightly longer range, from nineteen to twenty-nine. Except for two English women, they were all American-born, predominately easterners, and, interestingly enough, the nineteen-year-old came from New Mexico. Of the thirteen listed, two were widowed and two divorced, and they all lived in two defined districts in the town.

Durango, the twelfth census revealed, contained a larger district than most of the San Juan communities. The "sporting women," as the census-taker gently defined them (although for some reason two were called "mistress"), ranged in age from the twenties into the thirties, predominately in the former. They came from all over, including Colorado. Interestingly, ten were either married with no husband listed, divorced, or widowed. While some had children, none were currently living with their mother. Gamblers and saloon owners also resided in the Durango district.

At the south end of the San Juans, Durango made its debut in the fall of 1880, a "more picturesque and attractive site would be hard to find even in Colorado," and it gained a red light district almost over night.

The town's first newspaper editor, Caroline Romney, did not hesitate to chronicle the new community's red light district, a development she did not in the least think enhanced the town.

When the Coliseum, the "new and elegant theatre," held its grand opening, the *Record* hailed it as a magnificent place of amusement, but then Caroline decided that it did not provide the type of amusement to enhance the town's reputation. Why? It was near the red light district and she suspected the worst with its "wildness." It did not help when the Coliseum attempted to contain rowdiness by requiring "the boys" to check their weapons at the bar.

In August and September, 1881, Caroline took out after the "dives," including finding an opium "dive" doing a "very good business" with "night after night full of intoxicated victims." Why did not the board of health look into this situation? Then she reported quite a "rumpus" by two of the women. And then much to her disgust, most of the "gamblers and harlots" driven out of Silverton landed in Durango.

Frustrated that nothing was being done, she commandeered one of Durango's finest and led her own raid on the district to point out the problem. Yet even Caroline could become quite sentimental about one of the girls, Sarah Smith, alias "Maud Austin," who died. "She was a remarkably good-looking woman, and had a pleasant disposition, being affable to all, and consequently was a general favorite." A native of Indiana, Maud had been married but, "on account of domestic troubles," left home and came west, "to live a life of shame. Here we drop the veil of charity."

Caroline dropped the "veil," then quickly turned her attention to the Clipper Theatre, another "den of iniquity" that graced her town. She warned her readers, back on February 18, 1882, that parents should "look after their boys" and know where they "are in the evenings." The young, she cautioned, "are easily seduced by lights and music," and once inside the Clipper "every temptation to evils that are possible to imagine are placed in their way."

How bad was it? "Lewd girls are the chief attraction." They frequent the boxes before the play and "between acts are soliciting orders for the most degrading commerce, while the stage itself panders to the lowest instincts of human nature." She continually fretted and continued warning parents to know where their boys were in the evening. Even a curfew did not seem to help. Temptations lurked in Durango.

At the same time, one of Durango's other newspapers (the town had five in 1881-82), the *Southwest,* became very sentimental about "another tragedy." A "beautiful, graceful young mother" with a child was abandoned by her husband after he killed a man. She tried operating a boarding house but struggled against "poverty and dull times." Failing at that occupation, she "sank into the mire of prostitution" as the proprietress of a local brothel. Her "sisters of shame united in saying she had no business" being a prostitute, and she finally killed herself with morphine. The paper concluded, "So ended a life that might have been a joy and a blessing to all about her."

Durango faced another prevalent "evil" in 1886, opium. Apparently, several "opium dives" had been exposed the year before, yet nothing had been done about the "evil," except the "opium fiends" had become more cautious. Now, the "sodden sallow eyed opium wrecks are daily seen wandering aimless about our streets." Three years before, the *Durango Daily Herald* (November 22, 1883) had pointed out that the council recently had passed an ordinance regarding the issue that seemed to have done no good. Nor apparently had it since.

Finally, in 1886, the city closed "Jim Lee's stinking and detestable den," a place that "pretends to be a Chinese laundry." Not willing to stop there, the *Herald* reflected the typical anti-Chinese emotions of the day. Lee, the paper claimed, symbolized a "typical representative of the meek, lowly, cunning, vicious and depraved off-scouring of the Celestial empire."

While not yet understood in its totality, the Victorians understood that addiction to these drugs created a dangerous habit. Some critics blamed the Chinese because, after all, drugs had spread after their arrival in the United States. Already anti-Chinese rhetoric and violence against them stretched across Colorado. Only a few years before (October 1880), Denver had been the scene of a vicious and deadly riot; nevertheless the city was not alone. Pressure steadily increased to prohibit the Chinese from immigrating to the United States.

The typical newspaper story about prostitution and prostitutes continued to involve a certain amount of Victorian sentimentality, even in the case of suicides. There existed little glamour in a life of prostitution and the line. Reports from Telluride told of a "scarlet daughter" taking her life with chloroform. Silverton's Nettie Lewis took carbolic acid after her lover "concluded to drop her." She became despondent and committed "the rash deed." Durango's Clara Chase likewise "passed from earth."

Nonetheless, when Silverton prostitute Grace Marsh, "known in every San Juan town," committed suicide, "by administrating morphine," Rico's *Dolores News*, July 4, 1885, reported the event with few regrets but a dash of humor. The acting coroner summoned a jury, which heard the evidence and was about to pronounce a verdict when the doctor exclaimed, "hold on she's alive." Indeed she was. The jury promptly adjourned until the afternoon, "when they came together again and found she really was deader (sic)." "Her husband," Bill Marsh, "also quite well known in Rico, was wired (telegraphed) at Robinson" (a mining camp near Leadville), but it was learned he left there and his present "where abouts is unknown." It was not unusual that a prostitute had a "husband" who also frequented the red light district, and the term "husband" might, or might not, represent a marriageable relationship.

Dave Day, in his *Solid Muldoon* (January 15, 1886), described for his readers, with his usual humor, an attempted suicide by "one of the despondent daughters of prosperity who 'took a fit of blues' and with it a dose of cold poison in the shape of morphine." Thanks to "mustard administered in heroic doses," the soiled dove "was brought back to this practical world." He concluded his story, "at last reports she had braced up and was willing to remain with us a while longer."

Telluride Cribs, 1984
Courtesy of Duane A. Smith

Day could and did wax sentimental in his reporting. In September 1889, an abandoned, friendless, sick woman in Ouray was in desperate need. No one among the respectable folks seemed to care. Who came to her aid? A "woman of the town, Carrie Lannell," nursed the sick woman and took in her three children. The woman and her baby died, but Lannell fed, clothed and kept the children "out of the gutter." All this launched *Muldoon* editor Day into a moralizing statement about people's attitudes and inhumanity to others.

Day's wife, Victoria, displayed much less sympathy with the "ladies of the evening." One day her little daughter came home and announced she had seen the "prettiest ladies." They smiled "at me," and "I said, 'Who are you? Oh... we are chippies!'" When Victoria told Dave, he promptly went to see the city council and, as a result, "red-light women were not allowed on the streets in the day time."

The same thing happened in Durango when the girls rode in carriages down the Boulevard. Since it was "the" street in the town, it contained the best homes. Editor Caroline Romney had declared the street a "monument to the energy, pluck and perseverance of that portion of the American people who constitute the planters of Empire." Now this activity threatened to besmirch that image. The erring sisters were summarily told to stay in their district west of Railroad Avenue. The editor of the rival *Herald* also breathed a sigh of relief when that threat to morality had been repelled. It did not last.

If it was not one thing it was another for the hard-pressed reformers. In his March 6, 1887 issue, the *Herald's* editor declared that "cigarette smoking and whiskey drinking prostitutes should be kept off the streets." Not finished, he concluded that the "matter of seeing them but seldom is too much."

Even towns that had acted quickly enough to segregate the girls by ordinance might find themselves in trouble when the girls left their assigned district. The good people of Silverton, particularly those living in the vicinity of 14th and Snowden, became "very much scandalized" when a couple "not regarded as highly respectable to say the least" became their neighbors by renting a house.

Silverton's *La Plata Miner*, on December 13, 1884, became "greatly scandalized" by a disreputable woman. She went to the front of her house and in a "voice loud enough to be heard a block away" commenced "blackguarding everybody in the neighborhood." She hurled the "vilest epithets" and filled the air with "obscene language." The aroused editor promptly chastised the city authorities for tolerating this "disgrace to the fair name of Silverton."

Telluride folks likewise were shocked in early July 1886. According to the *Republican*, a "male party" engaged a room at the Watson House. He "surreptitiously occupied the apartment overnight with a frail sister from one of the sporting houses." Then he had the "gall to walk out without paying the bill." Finally caught, he had to "fess up" and pay.

While the red light district often proved the center of crime, the girls became victims as easily as their clients. Silverton reported a case, in December 1884, where an intoxicated girl "was relieved of $148" while drunk. She accused two of the other girls, Broken Nosed Nell and Mag

Davis, only to have them prove "their innocence." Eventually her "lover" was found to be the guilty party.

The girls often were victims of abuse, either by their pimp or lover, or perhaps by a client. Such events did not make the newspaper, or even perhaps stir any criminal investigation. Prostitutes lived in a world where, while tolerated, they were generally segregated as much as possible from the rest of the community. Their lives passed unnoticed, unless something happened that caught the local newspaper's attention. It seemed that out of sight meant out of mind.

As the 1880s came to a close, the San Juan communities began to review the prostitution issues, like their newspapers, with a sentimentality that must have helped make it seem, at least to them, more acceptable within the community.

For example, recall the suicides of Clara Chase and Nettie Lewis. Those instances offered the opportunity to discuss the negative side of the red light district and its impact on the women. In both cases, however, the editor forsook that opportunity and instead turned to Victorian sentimentality, which was so typical for the era.

For Clara, the *Morning Durango Herald* (March 29, 1887) sentimentalized. "Clara Chase is dead. Another gone wrong in life, over whose acts we draw the mantle of charity, hoping before Him who rules she may find the forgiveness for her fall on earth for which she prayed with her dying breath." Of Nettie, the same newspaper (July 26, 1889), eulogized, she was "fairly educated, very lady like in her deportment", and showed "evidences of having been well raised." All that might have been true, but the "woman of easy virtue" would be quickly forgotten, as life rushed on. No real lesson was learned or understanding reached about the situations that often forced the Claras and Netties into the red light district. Nor did the personal degradation seem to gain sympathy.

Dave Day appeared to adopt a double standard when stories involved local men and prostitutes. For example, in the *Solid Muldoon*, April 12, 1889, one such story was printed. It seemed one of Ouray's young professional men went riding with Florence. He accidentally fell from his horse and suffered an injury, but his name was not mentioned "for the protection of his mother." That did not stop Dave from identifying Florence.

This was not the only example of a double standard when it came to bordellos, demimondes, and their customers. When the "Hanging Gardens of Babylon" burned down in Durango, some of the town's prominent "young blades" came running out of the establishment carrying their trousers. Were their names mentioned? Not at all. So it happened in Victorian America, the patron escaped public censure, but the soiled dove did not.

The Victorians could be hypocritical about such issues. In fact, sometimes young men were encouraged to go out and sow their "wild oats" with one of the girls. Their parents would shun both the girls and the parlor houses and cribs, while privately condoning their sons' behavior; far better to do that than get a young, respected woman in a "family way." Again, it was the case of the baby crib (that symbol of the Victorian family) versus the red light "crib" and the role of mother and wife versus those seldom-mentioned sexual drives that proper young ladies "obviously" would not have or condone. Sex focused on procreating the human species and was definitely not for pleasure. Or, so some marriage manuals of the time preached to their readers.

Fascinatingly, where were the protests about red light districts in the San Juans? In other sections of the country, churches and women's groups opposed the institution much as they did the saloon. No doubt, ministers and women worked behind the scenes to try to rescue some of the girls. However, they faced a hostile public in the male dominated mining world about them. Not just from those utilizing the services of the district, but merchants and others who were loath to abandon such a profitable business and community attraction.

No doubt there existed silent partners and investors in the town reaping profits from this immoral trade. As long as times remained good and the profits rolled in to one and all there seemed no need to get too reform-minded until public pressure became too great.

Regardless, prostitution had taken root throughout the mountain mining communities. Rather than it being considered a good sign of reform, the departure of the denizens of the district was generally heralded as the first sign of the passing of the boom days and the coming of eventual decline. Sooner or later that eventuality came to pass to one and all in the mining West.

4

Times They Are A Changing
Prostitution in the San Juans,
1890s-1900s

As the decade of the 1880s ended and the 1890s made their bow, change was coming to San Juan mining and the region's communities. Silver had been queen, but its reign was nearing an end. In a sense, it had been subsidized by the Federal Government, which was purchasing the metal for coinage (thanks to two acts—the Bland Alison and the Sherman Silver Purchase). Silver's fate, however, hung not on Washington's action but on the world market. The world market was dwindling, as countries switched to the gold standard, and the use of silver coinage steadily declined. Since there existed, at that moment, few other major uses for silver besides coinage, a silver surplus came to pass to the dismay of silver miners throughout the West.

To make matters worse, Colorado and other western states continued mining silver at nearly record levels. As a result of this over supply, the price of silver declined from $1.35 an ounce to 90 cents. Cries of anguish and betrayal came with the crash of 1893 and the cruelly lingering depression that followed. Silverites in the West, who had long been agitating for a federally backed guarantee of silver's price at 16 to

1, or sixteen ounces of silver being equal in value to one of gold (valued at $20 plus change), found themselves marching out of step with their countrymen.

Easterners, politicians, and others blamed the economic woes on the government's silver purchase, and, in a special session of Congress during the bleak fall of 1893, ended the support for silver. The price quickly collapsed to fifty cents an ounce. Silver was done for, and so were many of the San Juan camps, which soon became "ghost towns." Among the San Juan towns, Rico, Lake City, and newly-opened Creede suffered the most. Silverton, Ouray, and Telluride fortunately mined gold as well as silver and continued to prosper. Durango, with a broader based economy, suffered too but survived.

All this chaos had an impact on the patrons of the red light districts and on the business of the "hookers," a term now more commonly used for the "scarlet sisterhood." In the towns, however, the pattern of the previous years continued, despite the depressed times.

Creede, in the early 1890s, boasted a red light district with a new twist. The notorious con man, Jefferson "Soapy" Smith, gained control of the district, as no other individual had ever done in the San Juans. His "reign" proved short, when the boom days ended with the crash of 1893. A visitor to Creede at this time left an unflattering account of the ladies of the line. He said that the women who frequented saloons and gambling houses "are the most unpicturesque." Furthermore, they "are neither dashing and bold nor remorseful" and an "unrepentant and unattractive element."

A *Rocky Mountain News* reporter, January 19, 1892, concurred. He described them as the "discarded remnants" of "old fairies who flaunt around in their (dance halls) as never were seen before." Nor did the negative description stop at that point. "The aforesaid fairies are not of the young, charming kind. They are a job lot of weazened witches."

Another Creede visitor also painted a most unattractive picture of one of the "daughters of Eros." She was "anything but attractive personally." Of short build, inclined toward plumpness, she had a "ghastly complexion." To add to this portrait, she "dressed slovenly, used no rouge or did anything to enhance her appearance," and had a "churlish disposition."

Neither were they immune to violence. Margaret Miller provided information about a murder in North Creede that occurred early in the twentieth century. Her father, a physician, was awakened one night at 2 a.m. by someone pounding on his door. A stranger told him a "woman had been hurt in North Creede and you are needed." So he dressed and left home.

> As he went up Main Street the saloons were lighted, but beyond that there was total darkness. At last in North Creede, he saw one house where all the lights were shining. He knew it was a notorious brothel. There was no one in sight, no one answered his knock at the door, and when he let himself in, he found a half-naked woman sprawled on the couch. Her body was covered with blood and she was dead—stabbed with a pair of shears.

An investigation eventually found that she had been murdered by another woman in the same house. "Saloon men put up money for her defense and stood by her during her trial and she was acquitted."

Suicides, or attempted suicides, continued dominating newspaper stories. For example, the *Mancos Times*, in its July 7, 1893 issue, reported goings on in the neighboring town of Rico:

> Two more unfortunates weary of breath rashly importunate gone to their death—a courtesan and a male restaurant waiter. All this happened in Rico last week and morphine was the chosen route. A second scarlet daughter started over the range on the same trail but was headed off by emetics and a stomach pump.

A woman who lived in Creede remembered the "wicked women of the town" more favorably. When a fire broke out, she rushed about, getting ready to move her things. Then came a knock at the door. "Three women of the demi-monde" stood there ready to help her. They said to "forget who they were and tell them what to do. I felt most grateful to those poor outcasts, and would gladly have treated them with kindness, but they never saw me again. Gave me no chance to speak to them." To her, "these people of the half world were never presumptuous, loud or boisterous in public places."

Ouray, meanwhile, faced trouble keeping the "daughters of joy" corralled in their district. A particularly troublesome time occurred in July, 1899. Numerous complaints reached the council about the "Pasqual Saloon with female rooming" on the second floor.

> Women are at the bottom of all this trouble. Screens on the windows have prohibited them from exposing their anatomy to passersby, and a little vigilance on the part of the police committee has had a tendency to take them off the sidewalks...

Nearby saloon men protested that the women were not supposed to be on 3rd Street and requested that they "be removed from 3rd to the reservation allotted prostitutes on 2nd St." One saloon man stated that "if all were not treated alike he would send to Chicago to get six of the most beautiful women in the country to go into the 'rooming house business himself.'"

Finally, in August, the city council, fire, and the police committee investigated and reported back that all "soiled doves had winged their way (back) to the reservation." They thought the "nuisance entirely abated."

Prostitution, meanwhile, continued to supplement the revenues of San Juan towns. According to the *Silverton Standard* (November 4, 1893), for example, the town mayor required that it be accomplished on the sly.

During his term of office (John Wingate) was instrumental in compelling the sporting women of the town to pay a certain portion of the proceeds of their nefarious occupation into the town treasury. It was not in the nature of a license, because the law strictly prohibits the existence of houses of this character.

The mayor "directed" that the resolution not be recorded, as it was illegal. Yet, the muckraking editor would have none of such shenanigans and let loose with the following blast:

Now what was the object of the enforced contribution referred to? It would appear that it was incidentally to establish a high moral reputation for some one, and directly to decrease somebody's taxes at the expense of the unfortunate fallen women, in a manner repugnant to the feelings of any right minded person, and in direct violation of the law. We would ask the voters of this county, how many of you desire to have your taxes paid with such ill-gotten gains, and thus your action in accepting the process of a criminal act, place yourself in a position to deserve the contempt of even the prostitute.

The editor was on the right track, for the times were changing and the wild past was slipping into yesterday.

At the same time, another pattern was emerging in the San Juans; prostitution was beginning to be controlled by one family or a crime syndicate. Large cities throughout the country had already witnessed this development, with its varied implications.

Ouray, perhaps more than any of its neighbors, experienced this development. The Vanoli clan ran Ouray's red light district. They also became involved in Telluride and some of the smaller mining communities. For a while, the Italian underworld controlled Silverton's

Blair Street. The girls, games, and saloons were where the money was, and criminals naturally gravitated toward it. As the twentieth century approached, the San Juans more and more reflected aspects of the rest of the country.

The turn-of-the century found Telluride to be the San Juans' number one mining district and town, trailed by Ouray, Silverton and finally Creede. The other communities looked more to their past than to the future. Telluride, in fact, had emerged as one of Colorado's and America's great mining districts and the bellwether for the San Juans for nearly the next two decades.

Prostitution flourished in the community. The cribs and parlor houses thrived on Pacific Avenue right outside the railroad depot. That location upset some of the townspeople, as it did in Durango, with its district located on the south end of Main Avenue across from the town's depot.

Telluride's *San Miguel Examiner* and the *Journal* were not remiss in covering events in the red light district, some in jest, some seriously, and a few by moralizing. Those walking down the street, and especially visitors, as one Telluride resident observed, "nearly always wanted to walk through that section and peek in on variety theaters and dance halls." One wonders if they vicariously enjoyed a moment of being near sin as they passed the cribs; or were they tempted to sample the favors of the scarlet women themselves? Did they know that the red lights "are dimmed" only when the girl was entertaining a visitor?

The following quotes illustrate the ins and outs of the district, along with impressions of the girls and some of their customers, as viewed by Telluride's newspapers:

> What do you think of a white man who can get so stuck on a colored prostitute as to kill her because she prefers one of her race? Is there any punishment severe enough for him? *October 30, 1903*

Inside Telluride Crib
Courtesy Homer Reid Collection

One of the girls from the tenderloin district was a passenger on the morning train bound for outside points where healing water and doctors who are specialists will look after her case. A subscription was taken up for her among the denizens and frequenters of her district, who are, by the way, very sympathetic, generous and kind to one in distress, and in that way she was permitted to go out. There is little use to moralize to such matters, but it does seem that the downfall of one of these unfortunates might tend to make (an) announcement about the calling. Such is life, however.
April 6, 1906

One of the girls from the red light district was fined $50 and costs by Police Magistrate Holmes for being drunk and disorderly. The judge must have struck his gait again. *March 29, 1906*

All sorts of doings around the tenderloin district. The City Dads (have been) curtailing customers around these resorts. *July 4, 1908*

Annie Grant, one of the old time women of the half world, was adjudged insane in the county court this week and committed to the asylum at Pueblo. *May 23, 1908*

Two of the women from the red light district are languishing in the city jail today as the result of imbibing too freely and an inability to restrain their angry passions while carrying a load. They will be before the police magistrate this afternoon on a charge of drunk and disorderly. *Undated Telluride newspaper*

Maude Coy, a poor unfortunate, died yesterday morning in the red light district. She has a mother living in Denver, who has been communicated with and the funeral will be held tomorrow. *December 19, 1912*

Mining man Robert Livermore was in Telluride during the good times after the turn-of-the-century. He recalled it vividly and explained a reason why the red light district was allowed to flourish.

The town was wide open. I believe there were thirty-odd saloons, in most of which a roulette wheel and faro game were established. The feeling among the mine operators was that the sooner the miner got broke, the sooner they went back to work. The 'row,' near the river and railroad track, was inevitable, a feature of all mining camps of the day.

At the same time, labor wars broke out in Telluride and Cripple Creek, another of Colorado's major mining districts, and the National Guard marched into both towns in 1903-04. This time of troubles spelled the end of the free-wheeling days. As was typical for the time, the owners emerged victorious and the miners union lost.

The *Telluride Journal* made several observations about the troopers, the district, and the girls. The combination equated to trouble waiting to happen.

About midnight Saturday night a fusillade of revolver shots startled the town and the shooting came from down on the flats in the red light district.

The provost marshal and his patrol made a hurried investigation and found that about a dozen soldiers, crazed by cheap whiskey surreptiously (sic) procured from some of the lower class saloons, were giving an exhibition of their assininity by terrorizing the denizens of the flats by entering houses and cabins and shooting off their revolvers.

Of the dozen troopers arrested for the disturbance of Saturday night, only seven are held for court-martial, investigation showing that the others were not implicated in the demonstrations farther than being of the party....

The militia officers and the (rank and) file generally regret the circumstance exceedingly, as well as the entire community. *January 28, 1904*

The bawdy houses of the red light district have come under the military and all were closed up tight Monday night with instructions to stay closed. *February 4, 1904*

As soon as martial law ended, the district reopened and trouble resumed, the underlying tensions not being resolved.

Rumors are rampant today on the streets that denizens of the red light district had best have a care in their actions on the streets, and treatment of frequenters of the resorts, else they will be jerked up by the strong arm of the law and places closed permanently. A great many of their vices have come to the public eye which should be confined to the resorts, and people have commenced to talk. Only today one of the inmates was arrested and jailed for being drunk and disorderly on the street. Better have a care. *Telluride Journal, May 23, 1907*

Occasionally, the town council did react to district disturbances. In a Telluride special session in March 1910, the city fathers revoked the liquor licenses of two saloons. Why? On account of the "difficulty the police have been having with denizens because of disorderly conduct."

Across the mountains, over in neighboring Ouray, that town's district was not any more peaceful and orderly.

Ouray had quite a serious cutting affray about midnight Monday night. A burro puncher, Clarence Templeton by name, with a somewhat tough disposition was taking in the red light district. So were several others—this being a popular Ouray diversion—among them one

Clinton Buskirk. They met in a dance hall and Buskirk dunned Templeton for $1.50, which he said Templeton owed him. Then Templeton drew an ugly knife from his belt and began slashing Buskirk right and left.

Templeton is in jail and Buskirk in the hospital with the outcome of his injuries still a matter of doubt. *Telluride Journal, March 5, 1903*

Silverton joined the news, again as reported in the *Telluride Journal* (April 9, 1908). Perhaps the editor enjoyed discussing the tribulations of a neighboring community. For whatever reasons, this Telluride newspaper proved a great source of red light district information from throughout the San Juans. For example, the *Journal* related this story about Silverton. Apparently the editor of Silverton's *Weekly Miner* took the town board to task, charging it with "unlawfully collecting fines from fallen women." The city fathers promptly responded by ceasing to "collect fines hitherto collected from prostitutes. Thus a considerable source of revenue is cut off from the city." Again, the story proved familiar, but "there is no record of the proceeding." That comment provided a rather interesting commentary on the times.

Rarely did murders happen, but, when they did, it became front page news and the talk of the town, particularly when the victim was a law officer. The *Telluride Journal*, August 4, 1910, emotionally headlined a shooting: "Popular Telluride Police Officer Foully and Cowardly Slain While Performing his Duty—Murderer Escaped and Is at Large--$1,500 Reward Offered."

The murder occurred in the red light district and stemmed from a confrontation in the Cosy Corner saloon. "The death of the marshal came as a distinct blow to many. The sympathy of all goes out to his relatives in this sad hour who all live in the east." The reporter also worried that they "can hardly be expected to judge otherwise than this is an example of the wild and wooly west of years gone by." The "Old West" obviously seemed no longer an attraction in the twentieth century— times were changing here too.

The district and the girls found themselves a political issue as well. Candidates in the Creede municipal election of 1913 felt obligated to place an advertisement in the *Candle, March 22, 1913.*

> In view of the numerous misstatements, mis-representations and malicious gossip now being presented to the citizens of Creede by the mouth to mouth process, the undersigned candidates for aldermen desire to set down here with FACTS accredited to them by persons opposing the PEOPLE'S PARTY.

They had been charged with "advocating the re-establishment of houses of prostitution," favoring "open gambling," and allowing saloons to "run wide open." They forthrightly replied they had not. "We believe in the enforcement of state and city ordinances governing these issues." They favored other forms of amusement, "especially social dances and moving picture shows," which "are essential and agreeable to a majority of our citizens."

Telluride's red light district inhabitants, meanwhile, managed to get in repeated trouble, even when innocently sleighing. The *Journal* (January 18, 1906) reported:

> A sleighing party of men and women from the red light district this afternoon got pretty boisterous upon leaving town and on their return marshal Runnells intercepted them as they were passing the city jail and locked the whole party up. There were three men and three women in the outfit.

Racism surfaced as well in reporting about district "goings on." When fire burned down two of Telluride's buildings, it was written that "the places have for years been utilized by colored prostitutes, and the neighborhood is known as 'Coon Flats'and is in the very heart of the toughest district of the town."

As stated previously, as the twentieth century moved ahead, the *Telluride Journal* seemed to be the only San Juan newspaper that was regularly reporting on the red light district and its girls. Telluride readers were tempted to read an article headed "Given a Chance to Reform": "One case of vagrancy was up before Justice Updegraff this morning." The affair involved a local young man who occupied "a position with a well known firm. His arrest was brought about through his habit of hanging about saloons, gambling houses and the red light district, and squandering his money." The fine and costs would be suspended "during the good behavior of the defendant and his promise to keep away from these places in the future." *September 10, 1908*

No matter the time, it continued to be unacceptable to seduce an "innocent young girl." Edward McDaniel, "who gyrates between thumping a dance hall piano and living off the shame of fallen women," was arrested for "the seduction of a 15-year-old girl," editorialized the *Silverton Standard, March 29, 1902*. The newspaper continued that "on account of the revolting nature of the crime, (McDaniel should) be billed for a long engagement at the penitentiary should he prove to be the person."

In the meantime, the newspapers started printing editorials, letters, and articles against that "social evil," prostitution. When a Silverton minister, in July 1895, preached a pointed attack against the evils of the day, the editor of the *Standard* wholeheartedly applauded and agreed. "It is a pity that all Silverton was not there to listen to the sermon and better still to practice it." After discussing "breaking every commandment," including stealing, bearing false witness, and worshiping false idols, the reverend hit upon the red light district.

There is anything and everything but a holy Sabbath. The commandment, 'Thou shalt not commit adultery,' appears to have gone out of fashion, but the harlot in silk is no better than the prostitute in calico and the commandment is for men as much as women.

A letter writer to the *Silverton Standard* on January 16, 1897, followed suit and protested against a double standard for women and men. "Perchance during a moment of thoughtfulness or passion she yields to temptation and falls from virtue." Then, women of "the so-called best society will spurn her presence as they would a viper; not offering a helping hand to raise their poor fallen erring sister."

The double standard of the day clearly was shown. Why would "they hold the erring brother, father, friend or acquaintance in the path of virtue and honor" and not "treat their sister who is unfortunate in not possessing much worldly goods with some degree of respect and equality? Do they? Let their actions answer."

The Woman's Christian Temperance Union entered the fray when it launched a "rescue work" program, not for the hardened prostitute, but the youngster "who had just gone astray." Under the heading, "Save the Girls," the *Telluride Journal* of August 22, 1907, carried a long letter written in the best emotional Victorian rhetoric of the day, from Mrs. D. M. Hayes, the State Superintendent of Rescue Work. The epistle must have brought tears to the eyes of some who read it and, no doubt, aroused them to greater work for the cause.

> If it were your girls, now caught in the devil's snare; betrayed, perhaps, through the sweetest and best part of a woman's nature, her love and trust cast aside like a broken toy, what would you do?.... 'Ah, if I could shield her from the cruel gibes of the world, give her some little heart's ease for all the bitterness of her suffering, I would be so glad to do it!'

The Woman's Christian Temperance Union have put themselves in the likeness of parents toward the girls who have gone astray. With true mother-love they have gone out after them. They have given them comfort and helped when they most needed it. For over twenty years they have maintained the Cottage Home for this class of unfortunates.

Did it ever occur to you that many times a girl faces the fact that in all this wide, cruel world there seem but two places where she may find a welcome. One of these is the brothel; the other the grave. Small wonder if in her desperation she chooses one or the other.

The W.C.T.U. offered hope to those unfortunates and now needed "good people" to stand up and contribute to keep the life saving-doors open. "Over 1,100 girls have been cared for and given a chance. Again I ask, 'Is this worth while?'"

What happened to this request in the San Juans is unknown. No matter, the pressure mounted. Quoting an unnamed New York newspaper, the *Telluride Journal*, January 2, 1913, started the new year off with another article that laid guilt on the district participant—and even more so on those who allowed it to flourish.

I want to say to the mothers that if their daughters have a nice little home of their own; no matter how poor, they are better off than the woman in the street, who has been brought down to degradation, while the man who is her partner in sin is received in society, and we women throw our pure daughters in his arms and never say a word. We are taught that it is a necessary evil. I say that it is an unnecessary curse. Who are the victims? Why our daughters, of whom a million out of those who are brought into the world die every four years, a prey to the effects of prostitution.

Even in the mining communities, the tide of public opinion now ran against the red light district. However, it took more than that to finally put an end to the district, as the reformers understood.

Certainly, when one who went wrong returned to the fold, that encouraged those struggling to put an end to the "painted women" and the assorted tribulations associated with the profession. Some girls got married or managed to break the "chains of sin" on their own. That was always cause for rejoicing. But then came the time to give another push against the other evils of the district and its participants.

Colorado, meanwhile, went "dry" in 1916, ending the career of one pillar of the red light district, the saloon. That institution never recovered, although, to be sure, the speak-easy temporarily offered sanctuary as a man's home away from home. The great experiment would eventually fail, and the drinking man entered a new world in the 1930s, when prohibition went the way of many well-intended reforms.

Along with drinking, another "luring evil," the dance hall, eventually disappeared. Long criticized and damned as a corrupter of young men and women, it would vanish and, like the saloon, never return in the same form. Ouray, caught up in a reform "wave," closed its dance halls. That marked, proclaimed the *Ouray Herald, May 9, 1902,* "the beginning of a new and more progressive era in the social conditions of Ouray." Why? "Dance halls are the product of new mining camps in the mountains or boom towns on the border of civilization, and Ouray has long since outlived the excuse for such institutions, if indeed, there ever was any."

Not finished, the editor continued piously onward. "All passengers in and out of Ouray are compelled to pass near the vicinity." The girls in "peculiar dress, rubber necking and goo goo eyes, gave all strangers a bad impression of the condition of society in the city." Not to mention that "chief" among the other reasons was the fact a "number of young men, many of whom are boys in their teens," frequent the establishments. Dance halls "give Ouray a black eye."

That reform effort did not help Telluride, though. The *Herald,* on May 16, quoted the *Telluride Journal* about related repercussions. Ouray's sudden improvement impetus had left its nearby neighbors holding the bag, so to speak. The "closing of Ouray dance halls dumped a lot of superannuated fairies and nondescript musicians" into Telluride.

Once the dance halls were closed, the council went so far as to order that no music be played in saloons or sporting houses. The gambling "hells" suffered the same fate, although gambling did not. People still liked to wager against the odds.

That left only the cribs and parlor houses remaining in the old districts. They too would eventually disappear in their old form. However, that would not happen all at once as Nellie Spencer's story aptly displays. Prostitution, per se, would not just fade away. Change would come with time, particularly as Nellie would say, when the "car became a mobile house of prostitution."

What caused this sudden reform? With the San Juan camps and towns declining, the red light districts no longer flourished as they once had. Flush times meant profit for the district establishments. Lean times meant farewell to easy money, customers, and the district itself. One indication of impending demise was the widening gap between revenues generated from the district and expenses for policing and controlling it.

The Telluride Times, September 12, 1907, offered this tidbit to its readers: "One of the largest sporting houses of the red light district has closed, the inmates, girls, pups, birds, etc. leaving for Cripple Creek a few days ago." Like rats abandoning a sinking ship, the disappearance of the girls provided a sure sign that times were changing. City treasurers probably bemoaned the development because of those long-collected fines. This disappearance of the red light district fines happened just as all city revenue started declining. City fathers had to start looking for new revenue sources, or they would have to curtail services.

Public opinion hardened against this social evil and many thought it a disgrace to fund the city in such a manner. As the W.C.T.U. illustrated, the fight against prostitution and red light districts was taking on a more aggressive stance. The district no longer would be considered a sign of prosperity and a "booming" town. It had become a social pariah in the changing times.

Given that the country was about to join "dry" Colorado and other states that had enacted prohibition and, in 1917, began sending troops to help its European allies make the world "safe for democracy" and fight a war "to end all wars" – it certainly seemed the appropriate time to clean up social messes back home. However, the end result would not be what the enthusiasts hoped and believed would happen, and the 1920s would drift far from their expectations.

Neither would the high times of mining nor the red light districts reappear. They had now become relics of a vanished past. Tourism had emerged as a potential revenue source for the old mining towns, a more respectable source without question. Indeed, in Creede, one reason to end the red light district was the negative effect its undesirable reputation might have on tourism. Eventually, though, the romanticized legend, not the reality, became a draw for many visitors. Thus the legend became the reality, and it would, remaining residents hoped, bring hints of prosperity back to their declining communities.

Nellie's Story

When I interviewed Nellie K. Spencer, she was ninety years old, slightly hard of hearing, and blind in one eye. As a result, the interviews (which took place between October, 1982 and May, 1983) were conducted by my writing out the questions and Nellie reading them. She would then proceed to discuss them or to expand on a previous answer. This sometimes led to some disjointed moments, but we both persevered. I soon learned not to jot anything down while she was talking, just to ask her about it later. She would politely stop and wait when I was writing, so I turned to making mental notes instead.

Physically, Nellie was not in the best of shape, but, mentally, she remembered well her days on the line. Rather interestingly, but understandably, one of the workers at the Four Corners Health Care Center told me that if any of the senior gentlemen caused trouble during the meals, the management put them at Nellie's table. She knew how to "handle men!"

Meeker, where Nellie grew up, is located in northwestern Colorado, in the White River Valley of Rio Blanco County. Named for White River Ute agent Nathan Meeker, who was killed in the Ute uprising (September 20, 1879), it had briefly served as a military post. The community grew in the years that followed, from 260 in 1890 to 507 ten years later, when Nellie remembered it.

A farming/ranching village, Meeker served as the business and political center for a vast, little-populated hinterland in that isolated part of Colorado. The community's highlight, during Nellie's era, probably occurred when President Theodore Roosevelt utilized it as his headquarters on one of his western hunting trips.

Nellie Spencer
Courtesy Duane A. Smith

This, then, is Nellie's tale, a story that she proudly told. There was no hint of regret, and, without question, she had succeeded in a life lived in the shadow of society.

My mother died at childbirth; I was born on October 15, 1892. My mother was a German, her name was Anna. My daddy came from France as just a poor kid, and he had a ranch and horses and all when he died. I was the daughter of a second marriage. I'm a mixture of everything. My Dad done everything: he drove a stage for a while, he had a team of horses, and he had a ranch. We had some horses and cows. The little calves were fun to play with—I remember them. We lived near Meeker. I'm a pretty good horseback rider too. I had a horse; we called him "Diamond," and he was a nice horse. I never went to high school. I went to a country school mostly. I haven't much education, but I got along pretty good without the education. I'm a pretty good shot: I've killed a deer. I know that country around Meeker—it's pretty.

My dad drove the stage to Meeker, and he stayed there all night. I lived in Meeker off and on.

Meeker was just a little town; everybody knew everybody else. Daddy had four acres down by the river, and we had a big log cabin with four rooms. I had a pretty good time; my daddy was good to me. He gave me hell in French, but I couldn't understand it.

My daddy was a little old Frenchman with a mustache, and he could cuss the dirtiest and the longest of any guy I ever heard. When he got mad, he got mad. My father, they called him "Frenchy"—not Jean, but Frenchy.

My daddy was a scout in the war with Indians, he got along well with the Indians, too. He told lots of big lies about it.

My daddy couldn't speak very good English, just French. Boy, did he mix them up, but life comes and life goes, doesn't it? It's what you make of it. My dad wasn't a very good farmer, but we made it. I loved the dog, the horse, and the little calves to play with. We had horses and cows. He sold them for a fair price, and I got a little money. I got along pretty good for a kid who didn't know nothing.

I was not a very good cowgirl. I loved horses, and I rode a lot, but I wasn't what you called a cowgirl. My dad's brand was the horseshoe.

I like horses. We had one big white stallion with a great big long mane. I'll always remember him. An old bachelor by the name of Billy Pile gave me that horse. He was some high class breed, I can't remember which. He just raised hell when he saw the mares. But I could ride him; he was tame. He got tangled up in the barb wire, and my dad shot him.

My other horse's name was Diamond. Diamond was a little white horse. And he used to act up a lot if he saw the lady mares.

I lived with a Methodist minister and his wife. They didn't have no kids, I don't think. I can remember him and her. I don't think he was a very good preacher, but he preached. I got a pretty good education there.

I went to church but I didn't pay much attention to the church. I guess it was there, but I was too young to care. That's where I got my religion, from him, which wasn't much. I guess I lived with them a couple of years. I think they went away, or my daddy moved me or something.

I remember the teachers; they were good gals, and we done the best we could. We didn't learn anything. My teachers were country girls, educated that way too, and I liked them. They were nice. I liked the country school—I learned how to read and write.

Think I learned more at home reading than I ever did in school, because it was a country school and we all run wild. That was it. You need an education in this world.

I used to go to country dances; wish I could do that now. We had dances in the old school house, with a fiddler. I could dance like a son-of-a-gun. And I loved it. (According to people who knew her, Nellie was a good dancer.)

I worked for about five months for one of the county officials after I finished school. He had lots of kids, but that was a tough job—too many damn kids.

My sister lived with a bartender and his wife who had a saloon in Leadville, and she was always with them. And my sister was pretty well raised. She got married and had a family; she was a pretty good girl. She was kind of high toned. Clare was her name. I only had the one brother, that's all I had. I don't know if he is living or not. His name was Clarence.

I left Meeker after my daddy died.

Nellie had very little to say about her husband, whom she married when "I was about twenty-three."

Ya, I got married just one time. My husband, his name was Herbert Spencer, died about five years ago (about 1977). We had a place down by the river. He was an Irishman, farm background. We got along good; he was a good guy. All Irishmen are good guys, I guess.

We lived in Greeley for a long time. My husband's folks were farmers. He was a wild farmer. He was one of eleven kids. He did a little bit of everything.

Regarding her husband's opinion of her occupation, Nellie made several observations.

No, my husband didn't mind—he was kind of sporting himself. He was a poor kid, you know. Us poor kids grow up, and we're kind of different.

Me and my husband would go to dances in Durango. We had a good time and maybe drank too much. I always rented a cab to take us home.

Looking back over her life, Nellie remarked:

I had a birthday last October, I'm ninety. I'm getting old; all I have left is a big mouth. I look old. I look pretty good for my age, when I'm all dolled up.

Nellie's birthday occurred during the series of interviews. My teenage daughter, Lara, had wanted to meet her, and did, and enjoyed talking to her. Nellie was quite the lady, when Lara was around. Knowing it was Nellie's birthday, Lara wanted to give her a gift. The director of the home told us that when Nellie received presents, she enjoyed the beautiful paper and never opened the boxes. She would, however, enjoy fruit and candy, if not wrapped.

So we went to the grocery store and selected some items we thought she might enjoy. On the way out, Lara picked out a large mint candy. When we gave the unwrapped gift to Nellie, she started to cry, which startled us to no end. She explained that, just the other day, "she had wished to her fairy" that she wanted a "big candy mint." That wish had been granted.

Despite her eventual occupation, Nellie's childhood reflected that of her contemporaries. There seemed little, at this point, that would indicate where she might cast her future. The teenage years, however, would tell a different story.

Nellie, apparently throughout much of her adult life, dabbled at writing poetry. She may have even had some poems published.

> We love the sound of the snow plows
> As they grind by
> We love the sight of a snow drift
> Twenty foot high.

Two "poems" (each with only one stanza) may give insights into Nellie and her life style. They were both titled "Pretending."

> I am only pretending
> Things are as they used to be
> I'm only just pretending it
> That you're still in love with me.

> I am only pretending I'm happy
> I am only pretending I'm gay
> With my tears so close go my laughs
> Sometimes they get in the way.

Nellie died March 26, 1984. Both she and her husband, Herbert, are buried in Greenmount Cemetery in Durango, Colorado.

A Working Girl

Nellie was about sixteen (ca 1907-08) when she made, for her, an amazing discovery—she could get paid for "diddling," as she referred to it. "I didn't diddle until I got older; then the diddling started (laughter). I think I was about sixteen before I ever started charging for it anyhow. Up to then, I gave it away (laughter)." That discovery obviously changed the outlook on her future and set the stage for the rest of her life.

During the series of interviews with Nellie, we discussed prostitution and her career. The following format reflects those interviews. I posed the questions, written out, as mentioned, because she was hard of hearing. Then she would carefully read them with her one good eye and would take her time when considering the answer. This chapter is organized in that arrangement.

She was never hesitant in answering a question. As far as she could remember, she gave the best answer she could. Indeed Nellie seemed to enjoy discussing her "career."

Nellie sometimes stayed with the question, but at other times, almost as often, she would wander afield if something else came to her mind. Most of those side comments have been left in their original responses, even if they may have nothing to do with the initial query. That better preserves the flavor of the interviews.

Throughout the interviews, she explained her philosophy of life, which can be basically summarized in two words, money and fun. As she admitted several times in the September 23, September 30, and October 4, 1982 interviews, she enjoyed the "sporting life," and "I always like money." She also added more than once: "You know, it was a good free life, though, as I look back on it. We had fun; we had lots of fun. Everybody had fun. We had money, clothes, and had a good time. You know for a sporting girl, life just goes on."

Then later, in the October 4 interview, Nellie came back to the "fun" topic again. "I had a lot of fun as a sporting girl. Fun is what counts in this world— you're having fun. I made money. Money was my king. I heard that from my father; he always said save your money. I got along good. I liked it okay; you got to be something when you're alone in the world." Finally, on December 9, she observed, "Life is life, and you can't change it. Well, it's a great life, if you don't weaken."

Nellie also made this observation on December 9, 1982: "You know, a red-light district is a good thing in a town. The men know where to go and what to do. The girls do, too." In that same interview, when asked what her hobbies were, she frankly said: "My hobbies were men (laughing)." Those comments seem as close as Nellie could come to expressing her life's philosophy.

The reader may not be in agreement with all of Nellie's observations or conclusions or her blunt "philosophy of life." They are hers, however, and she was quite positive where she stood on the various questions posed to her. As she observed in the October 28, 1982 interview: "I remembered things I should do and things I shouldn't do, and what I could get by with and what I couldn't. We're crooked too (committed crimes), you know (laughter)."

Obviously, over the course of the interviews, repetition occurred in her answers. These generally have been deleted, unless they

Nellie Spencer, c1920s.
Courtesy of Duane A. Smith

further illuminated her answers or perchance gave a new insight or interpretation of something she mentioned in another interview. Nellie enjoyed talking, and at her age could not always remember what she had discussed previously that day, let alone days earlier. The date after each question refers to the day or days of the interview(s).

Did you know any girls in the Red Light District when you were growing up? *September 23, 1982*

> I knew a lot of girls in the red light district when I was younger. They were all good girls; they were just making a living. I tried it too. Sporting girls are very friendly. They're used to mixing, you know; they have to mix to make a go.

Were the guys nice to the girls? *September 23, October 27, 1982*

There were a lot of nice guys, a lot of sons of guns, but I did okay. Well some were neat and some were mean; they're not all alike, you know. Some men treated you like a queen, and other men treated you like a dog, and that's the truth. Most men treated me pretty good; most men treated us pretty good. If they didn't treat me pretty good, I left them alone and that was that.

A lot of good looking guys came in. A lot we liked, a lot we hated; but we got along pretty good. Most of the guys were pretty nice to us sporting girls—they liked 'um. They figure they're the only ones they'll get acquainted (with) among the women. It wasn't too bad—we had a lot of fun. I guess that's the way they are yet.

(Later, on October 27, she elaborated.) Oh, we had trouble with them, a lot of trouble. Some of them were mean, but men were pretty good to a woman.

If we had trouble, we just left them alone, stayed away from them. Sometimes, if we were where we could call the cops, we did—if they mistreated us. The police gave protection to the girls most places.

If rowdy customers became a problem, how did you handle them? *September 30, 1982*

Oh, we just handled them and put up with them, I guess, if we had to. We generally had a bouncer to take them off of you. The bouncer kicked them out, he kicked them out. We got along pretty good that way;

we weren't abused, you know. We were a pretty crafty bunch, as a matter of fact (laughing).

Did you have a pimp? *April 14, 1983*

I didn't have no pimp. They had a regular district for the girls, they called it a district.

What problems did you encounter? *April 14, 1983*

Our main problem was keeping clean, not getting a dose you know, syphilis or something like that. That was the only bad problem we had, keeping clean. Too many of the girls got something wrong with them and died.

In what cities or towns did you work? *September 23, 30; October 4, 14, 27, 1982*

We worked wherever we seen a dollar—that's where we got it. We hustled in farming towns and mining towns and everywhere we could. We never passed up a dollar. At least I never did. I had money in the bank, when I was young, from hustling that way. We didn't draw strings (slang—who would open the "game," in this case apparently the girls did not wait for the customer to open the" game"), never, if we could get a dollar. We liked money; all sporting girls like money. If they didn't, they wouldn't be in the work. These old women (the ones boycotting Nellie at the home), especially the married ones, they ain't so damned nice. They're just women like we are.

I worked in saloons. We helped sell drinks. Some of us did it for the money and some of us didn't have to. We hustled a little in the saloons. Whether in a saloon or crib, we kept our money.

I worked a house, and I worked in a crib by myself. When you worked in a crib, you got all the money. We had a lot of fun. I wish I could have it again. Other girls didn't have it like we did; we really had a good time.

I got to Leadville a lot. Leadville was a good, live town. I don't remember much about anything, except Leadville. It has a reputation for having a lot of girls, sporting girls, you know. Leadville was considered quite a sporting town—lots of girls. I pretty near said "whore;" that's what we called them, you know (laughing).

(Nellie never referred to herself as a "whore"—she was a "sporting girl." When she used the term "whore," it was in a derogatory way.) "Whores" were those women who gave it away free in the backseat of a car. (Throughout the interviews, she had nothing good to say about that type of woman. In her mind they were more than competition, they had no "class.")

Responding to a question about ever being a madam, she said this:

I worked in parlor houses. We dressed better. The rest of us worked in what they called a crib. That's where I worked; you worked for yourself in a crib and got the money. (Nellie worked in both, as single girl in a crib, or a part of a group of girls in what she called a "rooming house.")

I never owned a parlor house. As I got older, I had rooming houses and kept a girl for the boys who came in. But that wasn't called a "sporting house"—that was a "rooming house."

Well, we were called "sporting girls," and we hustled wherever we could get a dollar. It didn't matter what town or where it was. Some of us went to church. I had religious training; I lived with a Methodist preacher and his wife for a couple of years.

I only remember a night or two in Denver when I was going through or something. We never missed anything if we could make a date. We worked whenever we could get it, but the night was the main trade. We wasn't particular, just so they had money.

Yes, I hustled in Telluride. We were under a doctor there: I forget his name, but we were under a doctor there. We had to go for an examination or he'd come. We were kept clean.

I never hustled in Silverton. (Nellie was unclear about that, she was in Silverton.) I don't know what I was doing in Silverton; I can't remember. I must have been doing something. I must have been hustling, because I had to eat (laughter).

(However, the following is how she responded to a question on April 14, 1983 about being a sporting girl in Silverton.)

Were you a sporting girl in Silverton? *April 14, 1983*

Ya. There was a lot of sporting girls in that town. They had lots of miners that come to see them to earn their dough. I remember them. You know miners love the girls; pretty much all men loved the girls though. You know sporting girls were respected in them olden days.

They (local women) didn't have anything agin 'em. They took care of the husbands and that was that. Then they didn't have to get messed up. They didn't have anything agin 'em. They figured it was a good deal.

Then the old man didn't have to mess with them, he had the sporting girls. A woman don't like for her man to cheat on her, but she don't like to give it to him when he wants it either.

Leadville. Leadville was a sporting town. Great doings in Leadville, Colorado. Drunken miners—I remember

Temple of Music, Ouray
Courtesy Ouray County Historical Society

them—and I mean drunk. It was a mining town, and everything was okay. I never worked in Cripple Creek.

I was never in Denver; I've been in Denver. Oh, I might have took a trick in a rooming house. We turned a lot of tricks that way. We'd get a room and we'd hustle the guy. We could charge them what we wanted to, and maybe we got it and maybe we didn't. We could go up in price, or we could come down (laughs); there was no law — you have a dollar if you need it, and you can get some more if you need it.

I didn't work a regular circuit or town, just where I wanted. I just run wild, and wherever I was, that was my place.

You know, I always liked money. I always had a dollar in my pocket. I could always keep a dollar; no matter how or where I got it, I could keep it.

I worked in cribs more than I did in a sporting house where there was a woman (a madam took a percent of each trick that one of her girls worked), 'cause in a house for yourself, you got all the money. That was pretty good; I wish I could do it again. And you know something? I never turned against men like a lot of women did. I like men.

Ya, I worked by myself. I never liked to share the old money.

You said you worked for a madam in a parlor house. *October 14, 1982*

Ya, I worked in a parlor house; so did a lot of girls. We roomed there, too, as I remember. We stayed there; we had a madam, a woman who was boss. We divvied up part of our money with the madam, you bet. You don't think she kept us for nothing. I forget how much they took, but I know they took quite a bit of the money. The madam did not furnish us with clothes, but maybe food, I don't remember. I know we always ate good. (Nellie added another statement, as she was apt to do. The question triggered something in her memory.)

We were a pretty good looking bunch of cats; they called us "cats."

Then you must have hustled in Durango? *November 23; December 9, 1982*

Well, when I first came to Durango, I did. I was in a rooming house, and I hustled in there. There was a big fat girl run it, by the name of Mary Morris. She had a rooming house, and I hustled there. You know, all them ladies used to be fat. I guess they ate pretty good (laughter).

I never worked in the Strater Hotel; I never did. They had girls, but they were call-girls—to call in. Hotels have got girls to call, you know.

Was Durango an easy town to hustle in? *December 9, 1982*

Ya, every time you look at a guy in Durango, he's ready (laughed). You have that kind of men here; they like women. All western men like women. Men are nice; I always liked men. I don't like women, but I do like men; I always did. Men always treated me better and were nicer in every way.

When you hustled, was there a period of time you would stay in town? *October 27, 1982*

As long as you needed to, you stayed, and it was generally pretty good. But some people moved around, like they do now. You get acquainted in a town, and you can make more money where you get acquainted and the men like you. I got along pretty good that way. That's all I knew, so I had to get along.

How much money did you earn as a sporting girl? *September 23, 30; October 3, 1982*

Well, different places we got different prices. It depended on the guy. Maybe we got a five dollar bill, maybe we got a twenty—it all depended on us, and we depended on the guy. We looked at the guy and charged accordingly. I liked the twenty dollars pretty good; them were the night dates. Here we stayed all night, night dates; I wish I could go through life again.

We got all we could get. You might as well put it that way. If we considered we could get a twenty, we got the twenty. Sometimes we went for less. But I was not much for dates, night dates; they're kind of tough on a gal.

I was in the sporting life ever since I can remember. I never turned down a five dollar bill or a dollar. And I never got over it.

❧ *83* ❧

(She laughed, gently slapped her hip and said this.) If someone came by with a ten dollar bill, I don't know what I might do (referring to her present home)! (Then she continued.) "But you know, at my age, some of your parts wear out (laughed).

Over the course of the interview, we returned to prices and profits on several occasions. Each time, Nellie would remember something new. How much did you make per night? *September 23, 30, 1982*

> Oh, it all depended on how much we stole. Sometimes the pay was pretty darn good. Sometimes, if a guy had a lot of money, we got a hundred or something good. But generally it was just a price—the going price, how much it cost.

> They did not pay before we went into the bedroom— before we went to bed. That was the pay day for us gals (laughed). I'm not sorry I led the life I did, though; I'm telling you, I had a lot of fun—more than most women. Most women are cranky sons-of-guns. I don't think much of 'em. I don't have any fun now, God knows.

Did you ever bargain over the cost of a trick? How about tips? *October 27, 1982*

> Oh, ya, we could be 'jewed down' (laughing). Some boys gave us plenty; some boys were tight. We got extra money a lot of the time. You know something; men are very good to sporting girls. They're better to them than anybody else. I guess they figured they get what they wanted without argument. With their wife, they have to argue to get it, and sometimes they don't.

At what age were you when you entered the sporting life? *September 23;*
October 14, 27, 1982

> Well, that is hard to remember. I hustled, as far as I can
> remember. I think I was always diddling. Well, nobody
> bothered me. If a guy was nice to me, Okay, let him have
> some.

> I didn't need the money; I still hustled. It was a good
> life—we had a lot fun. Met a lot of nice guys—a lot of
> son-of-guns, too. But life goes by and is gone, and you
> wish you could do it over again.

> Well, I guess I seen the other girls do it, so I thought I'd
> do it to get money, some money. Sure, we loved money;
> we loved to make money.

At what ages did girls enter the profession? *October 14, 1982*

> . . . we were young. Heck, they had girls in the sporting
> houses that were 15, 16, wherever they could get them.
> The age didn't matter. If they were young, they were the
> better ones; they got more money. Maybe somebody
> took care of the older sporting girls, maybe they didn't.
> Well, they died.

Did you enjoy the sporting life? *September 23, 1982*

> Ya. We had a lot of fun. We had a little grief, too, because
> every once in a while we got a son-of-a-gun that was
> hard to put up with him, and took care of him. We had
> good clothes.

What about the police giving you trouble? *September 23, 30; October, 27, 1982*

Oh, sometimes. I've been in jail. They didn't keep me long. It was for hustling on the street, you know. I never liked being in jail. I was never a sporting girl in Durango, I was past the age. (Nellie contradicted this statement about not working in Durango on several other occasions.)

Oh, ya, all sporting girls had trouble with the law. I think I was in jail in Grand Junction once; they had a pretty good sheriff—I can't remember his name. I've been in jail. It ain't too bad—they treat you pretty good in jail.

I guess if we got in trouble, the men around took care of us, what we called pimps. Pretty near all of them had a man they called a pimp. I never had none of them. I was too mean (laughed). I don't know why I didn't; I guess I didn't want to be bossed around or bothered. (Apparently Nellie's husband did not pimp for her, or at least she gave no indication he did.)

You know, we had a license to hustle in them days. I don't know how we got it or anything about it, but we had a license. (She might be referring to a medical slip stating she had a monthly exam and was clean, or, in some towns, the girls purchased a license.)

We had to pay a fine in them towns where we worked. The landlady paid a fine, and the girls paid a fine. And the police come around regular and got it, and the police were more or less the boss, you know. So that wasn't too bad. We paid 'em. I guess the lady paid them plenty. They called it "protection."

Would you have to bribe the police? *October 27, 1982; April 14, 1983*

In a lot of towns, you paid to hustle; it was just like it was a business. If you didn't pay, you didn't hustle. But they didn't charge very much. We could afford it, I guess. You can bribe them or try to get by for free and get pinched (laughed). We called it pinch.

What about paying for protection? To whom? *December 9, 1982*

We did when we used to hustle at sporting houses. We paid. We paid for the privilege, and they took care of us, more or less. Some took a commission off the trick. That was the way they generally done. We had protection; the cops didn't get us (laughed)). You know, it's something, when you're working for a person and the cops don't get you. They get you for money, generally.

Do you remember any of the girls you worked with? *September 23, 1982*

I remember 'em, but I don't remember their names or where they were from or anything. Just a bunch of girls running wild, but we had fun. You know, that's the main aim of life—have a little fun and get something out of it.

Where did the sporting girls come from? *October 14, 1982*

Oh, we came from everywhere—little towns, big towns—we were there. I don't remember much about them; there were lots of girls.

Were you ever worried about becoming pregnant? *September 23, 30, 1982*

> Yes, I did. Well, I got knocked up once, and I took some medicine and got rid of it. I said to myself, never again. I think we had a preventive of some kind, but I don't remember much about it. I never wanted any kids. I sort of figured maybe the way I was, kids wasn't for me. I never had any kids, and I'm glad.

Would men come to you, or did you seek them out? *September 23, 1982*

> We just run wild and done as we pleased. Men came to us. When I got married, I had a good husband, a good-looking guy.

> Some men are ornery, some men are mean. They come in and stay with you and give you heck while they did. Most men were pretty nice.

Might you ever roll a drunk? *September 23, 30, 1982*

> Ya, we rolled lots of drunks, you bet your life we rolled 'em. All sporting girls roll drunks—that's what they're for (laughed). We used to get them drunk. We'd buy the booze and get them drunk, then we'd roll them.

Did you ever give a man knock-out drops? *September 30, 1982*

> No, I never had to. I was treated pretty good when I hustled, not too bad. You know, when I lived with that minister and his family, that kind of took with me a little and helped me a little to be half way good.

What about the clothes a sporting girl wore? *September 30, 1982*

> Yes, we dressed pretty nice. That was part of the game, to be dressed nice.

> We could go anywhere to shop. They were glad to see us—we had money.

How long were you a sporting girl? *September 30, 1982*

> Well, I never did quit it entirely. Not until I got down, you know, where I can't. I always hustled—we called it 'hustling', you know.

Would the men usually drink with you? *September 30, 1982*

> Ya, they were supposed to purchase us a drink. Doggone it, we drank (laughed).

> I drank mostly whiskey, kid, not beer. Beer wasn't strong enough (laughed) for us gals. It didn't look good. If we went to the bar, we paid for our drinks. I paid for drinks, you bet.

Did you like to dance? *September 30, 1982*

> Ya, we all liked to dance. In the dance halls we all danced; we danced with anybody we wanted. The men didn't pay for every dance; we made our money mostly in the bedroom, you know. Some places they paid to dance every dance. We had both regular and square dances.

What about card playing? *September 30, 1982*

> I played cards. We did everything we shouldn't have (laughed). You lost your money sometimes, and that wasn't good. They had big card games in those days, the men did. A lot of card players.

Would you enjoy sex with customers? *October 4, 1982*

> Well, not too much, a little bit, not very much. I don't know, I was always cool that way. Once in a while, but not very much. It was kind of business with me, from the time I started, to make money to get something to live on. I always worried, when I was young, of wanting something to live on.

> Of course, I had a good time once in a while, but it was business. I liked the money, and I kept a lot of the money you know. That's the reason I can be here (at Eventide) now and have a little care.

Were you ever instrumental in helping any girl to become a sporting girl? *October 4; November 23,1982*

> Well, I can't say I helped them; no, I never did. We were just all together, we were sporting girls. A sporting girl was considered something in them days. You know when you're young; you think that is really something. As you get older, you know darn well it wasn't something. As you grow old, time is gone, your life is gone and you know it.

Looking back, do you regret being a sporting girl? *October 4, 1982*

No, I was left alone—I just run wild. I done pretty good, though, for a girl that wasn't raised to know nothing.

Sporting girls are sometimes accused of being drug addicts. Did you use drugs? *October 4, 27, 1982*

I never used drugs, I never did. I never went for drugs. I always figured I was dumb enough without taking drugs.

Some of the girls go on that; I never did. The cost depended on where you took it, and where you got it. Some of the men who had it were crooked, too, you know. I always kept in pretty good condition and took care of myself and tried to be a lady, even though I was a sporting girl. Even for a sporting girl, I never got nasty or vulgar. I never did. I didn't smoke, and I only drank once in a while. I kept pretty clean for what I was.

Did you pay a doctor for a monthly visit? *October 14, 1982*

Ya, we always paid our doctors—I don't know whether in advance, but we paid him. And I think authorities paid him to look after us and see that we were kept clean and didn't burn them all (clients). We were given a certificate to put on the wall to state we were clean (laughed). It was good for the first client.

What about the doctors who treated you. Did they ever get into trouble with the police? *October 27, 1982*

Well, I guess some of 'em did. Some of 'em were careless, and maybe the girls died or got sick or told on them.

I always got along pretty good with everybody. Some people were scared to death of the police; I'm not scared of the police. If they get me, Okay.

How about parties on Christmas and other holidays? *October 14, 1982*

Yes, we took the holidays. We had a heck of a time on holidays. Business was good on holidays. The old boys come in.

Were you welcome in towns? *October 14, 1982*

We were welcome. Sporting girls didn't used to be snubbed or anything. We were considered all right. We had money and when you had money, you were somebody. And that goes for today.

You did not use your real name when you were a sporting girl. Why? *October 14, 1982*

No, we had a different name in each town (laughed). Any name—I don't remember the names I had. I know I took the name of Iris. I still use that name—it stuck with me.

Would sporting girls own or rent their cribs? *October 14, 1982; April 14, 1983*

Well, we rented them generally—we rented the cribs. We paid a pretty good price: I don't remember what, but we paid for 'em. You know, in olden days a sporting girl was something. They ain't nothing now but trash. But they were something when I was of age. We did a lot of good in the world—I won't say what (laughed).

We never lived in the cribs that I remember. (She forgot she had.) I think we all had a room or something—a room, I guess.

(She later explained in her own innumerable way) We kept the old man off the old woman! Women didn't look down on us; they considered us a necessity. We were needed, you know; that saved their hides (laughing).

I worked in a crib, little places by yourself. Just one man at a time came into the place, them was cribs. There were a lot of them at Leadville and different towns you know. It was better than a whole gang of girls at one time.

Was there some way a man might know if a sporting girl was by herself in her crib or with a customer? *October 14, 1982*

Well, I guess we just told him or something; we didn't have little signals or anything like that. If they go in, it was open; if they didn't, it was shut.

Did you work and hustle in a saloon? *October 14, 1982*

I worked in a saloon where we sold drinks on commission. The gal who could sell a lotta drinks was pretty welcome there.

Oh, sporting girls were hustlers. Oh, we hustled everywhere; we never passed anything up. We was hustlers—we hustled. We were better off than the girls are now, hustling the streets and alleys.

Would your customers use a condom? *October 14, 27, 1982*

I remember that they had them and used 'em. Not pass around disease or something. In some places we were under the doctor's care all the time, so we would be clean you know.

Well, I don't remember what contraceptives were available, but we had it, whatever it was. You could go to the doctor if you were pregnant and wanted to get rid of it or had diseases. They kind of had a special doctor for the girls.

What about the use of drugs or opium? *October 14, 1982*

Oh, ya, a lot of 'em used dope and everything. I don't exactly remember what kind of drugs, but I think they took shots in the arm. I never did. I never took a dose of anything like that in my life. The ones who had money and wanted them bought drugs. And they paid a good price too. I never wanted them that bad to put out my good money for 'em. I was a tight little son-of-a-gun (laughed).

Would you nurse any of the sick girls? *October 14, 1982*

No, we never done that. You know, sporting girls wasn't mean; we weren't mean. We took care of our business. A lot of the girls took care of their parents and everything—you know, with money.

The other women in town, did you get along with them? How did they treat you considering your occupation? *October 14, 27, 1982*

Some of them would treat you nice, just like anybody else. Treat you nice, or be nasty with ya. You know, decent women used to have a lot of toleration for sporting girls. They liked them because they figured we took them (husbands) off of them. We got along pretty good that way. A lot of married women hate to have the old boy go to bed, so if he can go out and get it, they let him go and they don't say nothing about it.

Now they kick a sporting girl in the hind end, but they didn't do it then. They despise us now, but it used to be they had a lot of respect for us. They figured we took care of the old boy. They want to be married; they want a guy to keep them and be nice to 'em, but when it comes to diddling, unhuh—they'd rather with a stranger, I guess (laughed). You know, it's a funny world, but you take it as it comes.

How about the merchants, did they treat your fairly? *October 14, 1982*

They treated us good; we had money. When you have money, you get treated good, I don't care. That's the same today.

What about pets, did you have any? *October 14, 1982*

We had pets. Mostly cats, because we could keep them in the house. Sure, they had names; I don't remember their names. I think we just called them pussycats (laughing). I always liked little dogs, little fancy dogs. I had some of them; I still like them. I think they're cute.

Were any of the sporting girls married? *October 14, 1982*

Oh, ya, a lot of them married down there. You meet women even today that were in the sporting houses, got married, and went decent.

You mentioned that you did not have a pimp? *October 27, 1982*

No, I didn't have no pimp. I didn't go for pimps; some of the girls did. But the pimps took the money and were mean to the girls; I knew better than that. I knew enough anyhow to save a little money. My dad was a little Frenchman from France and he said, "save your money, kid; you are your money kid."

How commonly were the men drunk? *October 27, 1982*

Well, yes, a lot of them were drunk; a lot of them wasn't. But even the drunk ones treated you good. You know, men are not mean. Men are not mean like women are; women are mean sons-of-guns in their hearts— men ain't. I've got more respect for men than I have for women. Sure, they go ahead and diddle, but that's nature. But they're better than women are; women are dirt.

Were there different types of sporting girls—high class and low class? *October 27, 1982*

Ya, we had high class ones, and ones that weren't so hot, and there were tramps; we called them "tramps." Just like anybody else that way, you know. We were women just like other women. Some liked men; other sporting girls don't like men. I always liked men. I always figured the men were always fair with you—pretty good that way. Women are crooked, and that goes for today, too.

Discussing the status of sporting girls, Nellie listened and then answered a question about smoking. *October 27; November 23, 1982*

> Oh, I tried 'em. I tried everything when I was young. Just the sporting girls smoked, not decent ones. You know, the decent girls were supposed to be decent.

Would sporting girls work a regular circuit? *November 23, 1982*

> I think all them little towns used to have girls. Took whoever come that had the money. You know, a sporting girl likes money (laughed).

When you were a sporting girl, did you work outside of Colorado? *October 27, 1982*

> No, mostly in Colorado. I stayed pretty close to home. I was young, and I was kind of scared, but I was careful.

Some girls worked in a dance hall? *November 23, 1982*

> No, I never worked in a dance hall. I know what they was. They dressed pretty darn nice; I remember that. They had a pretty good time in those dance halls— dancing, singing, piano playing.

One of the stories about prostitution was hanging a red light outside of your crib. Did you hang a red light bulb or lantern outside your crib? *November 23, 1982*

> I never did; I guess maybe the regular houses did, you know, but I never did. The regular houses did have a little light.

Was there a kind of music which helped attract business? *December 9, 1982*

Piano music was the main thing. We had some good players, too.

Nellie's neighbors in Durango were Mexicans, and, from the interviews with her, she found them to be very likeable. Nellie became the major land owner along Durango's Animas River frontage when she and her husband purchased her "crib" and additional properties in that area. She had this to say in a December 9, 1982 interview:

> I knew all the Mexicans, because we had four acres down there (along the Animas River, south of the Main Avenue Bridge) and had Mexican tenants. That was when my husband was living. We bought it (the crib in the red light district), and there was twenty-one houses, and we put all the white people out and kept the Mexicans. They all got along together. It was that way until he died, then I sold it all except the one place.

Considering the life they led, did any of the sporting girls you knew commit suicide? *December 9, 1982*

> Oh, ya, a lot of them committed suicide. I never got disgusted; I like money. A lot of them do commit suicide; they get disgusted, but I never got in trouble or got pregnant or anything, so I got along pretty good.

Photographs show many of the sporting girls being heavy set? *December 9, 1982*

> Sure, some of them were fat; everybody is fat sometimes (laughed). I was pretty fat, you know; I weighed about 140.

Did you have a good time as a sporting girl? *April 14, 1983*

> Sure. We had a heck of a time (laughing). We had a lot of fun and we got money too. You had good clothes and that was that. As I got older, I worked at sporting houses. It was better at getting money. It was a good life. Life ain't bad for a sporting girl. They have a lot of fun.
>
> We used to say men were all alike, and they haven't changed any. And they love to chippy around. I think it was a good thing when they had sporting houses for a man to go to.

Nellie made a series of general observations. *April 14, 1983*

> If you were a good hustler, you got a lot of trade.
> Ya, the girls went to church sometimes. I don't say it took a hold of them very hard, but we went to church.
> In olden times, men were the bosses, now I think women are the bosses.
>
> I think the sporting house was better than the women chipping all over town. It was better.

Summarizing her career as a sporting girl, Nellie observed. **October 14, 1982**

> We had a lot of fun. I wish I could have it now (laughed).
> We done as we pleased, had good clothes; we had money. Life was okay.

Looking back over her "hustling days," Nellie became philosophical about her life and occupation. *October 27, 1982*

You know, I'm not sorry for anything I did; I did the best that I could with what I had (laughed). You know everything wears out in time (laughed). Or did you know that (laughing)? We were respected, on the line where we had a crib or something, and we hustled.

I'm glad my hustling days are over. I've got a little money; I don't want for anything. I've got a trunk full of good clothes. What do I need with them?

It was a good life when I hustled; we had a lot of fun. I liked it. We had money and we had good clothes. We had more than the other girls who weren't hustling. I wish I could live it all over again. I bet I'd make a bigger mess out of it than I did (laughing).

But in a later interview, I asked Nellie: would you be a sporting girl, if you had your life to live over again? *December 9, 1982*

Well, no, I wouldn't. I'd get married and settle down, if I had it to do over again. You know, you don't make life, it comes to you.

And life did come to Nellie, but not without a few bumps along the highway. The negative part of a prostitute's life affected her as well as her contemporaries. This is revealed with the mention of kick backs, drugs, being shunned by "good" women, and the violence associated with the profession. The key to Nellie's survival is found in her statement, "it's a great life, if you don't weaken."

Nellie's Friends and Acquaintances As They Knew Her

Vera Lindsay, a longtime friend of Nellie's, added further insights into Nellie's true personality and life. She became acquainted with Nellie in the "very early" 1960s when she was working in a beauty salon. Vera, however, knew her as "Iris." She was interviewed on February 22, 1999.

Tell me how you happened to meet Nellie?

> I was working in Effie's Beauty Salon there on Main Street, and she came in and started being one of my customers, and she just stayed with me.

> She would come to the beauty shop, yes, she would get a taxi and come up there, and then she would have me call the taxi, and she would go back home.

We were talking about Nellie last week, and you said that Nellie had an abused childhood.

Yes, she did. She told me about it in later years. I didn't know about it for a long time. In fact, I didn't know Nellie for years, and finally she started telling me little things. And she said she was in an orphanage and from the time she was eight years on, they would farm her to the different homes and take the money, and she was abused then.

You said that she always had lots of money, that she kept it in a certain place.

Yeah, she did. She had a little cubby hole (where) she kept a lot of cash. She never paid anything by check. It was always by cash.

What do you think were some of Nellie's outstanding characteristics as a person?

Well, I think she was very kind. She was very caring. She was really intimidated by other people. She always felt like she was not as good as other people. She was always very friendly to me, but, now, she wasn't to most people. As far as I'm concerned she was a very remarkable individual.

What about her husband? Did she ever talk about him?

Yes, I know he was in some military service. I saw pictures of him. He was a very nice looking man, and he did all the cooking and cleaning at the house. She just ran the business.

From your experience, would Nellie seem to get along as well with women as with men?

No, because they pretty well shunned her. The people that had been there (the retirement home) for years, they didn't have much to do with her.

She liked children very much, but after a little while they would get on her nerves, you know, because she wasn't around them any.

Now you said she didn't get up before noon, and she wouldn't answer the phone.

She wouldn't answer the phone before noon. She would not answer the phone or go to the door before noon. They (Nellie and her girls) didn't get up until noon or so, and (then) they had breakfast.

People shunned her. She didn't go to the stores at all. She would call and they would deliver. She didn't walk down the streets. She came in directly from the curb when they would pull in.

Crowds bothered Nellie. She didn't like to enter into family groups, nor did she feel at ease in the holiday time like Christmas.

Nellie seemed to me to be an intelligent woman; was she?

She was very intelligent. Much more intelligent than the people of Durango ever knew. She would have been an excellent business woman had she been born in a later era. She certainly would have. She ran her business.

She had a very good sense of humor. You had to be able to talk to her though, and she didn't talk to many people. She had to get to know you before she would let loose and be what I think was herself.

She owned property along the river.

She used to own all the land up to the highway, up to what is now the by-pass and she sold some of it to the telephone company for a warehouse. She sold some to the power company for their offices and warehouse. So at one time she had a lot of property.

She loaned money to the Bank of Durango so it could open and also loaned money to some businessmen in Durango.

What was her home along the river like inside?

For that day, for that period, she had nice furniture. Today it would be worth a lot of money. It would have been a lot of antiques. She had a beautiful piano, and I ended up with the piano, and she had a lot of pretty things. She took pride in it. She wanted it all polished and kept clean and everything done.

You mentioned her husband and his role.

She didn't cook. Her husband cooked. They lived together, I don't know how far that living together went, but they lived there. He cooked for all the girls. I think he kind of worked for her in a way.

We talked about young boys who would run errands for her.

> She mentioned that some little boys would come and clean the sidewalk and go get the groceries and bring them back for her, deliver them, and she would always give them some money.

She must have been an interesting person.

> I know she liked to go down there (the Animas River) and fish. It was just outside her back door.

> She liked TV, and she did like to read. She spent a lot of time writing music. She had some of them recorded. I have a picture of the girl who did sing them, out in California.

> They were all real sad songs, like *I'm Lonesome for My Man.* Apparently, they didn't make the hit list, but I have several copies of them.

She never mentioned to me much about having any pets.

> She said, years ago she and her husband had a little tiny dog, and I saw a picture of it one time, a little fuzzy dog. But I don't know what happened to it. But she had some skunks down there that were her pets.

> She fed the skunks, she fed them warm milk and bread, morning and night. When I demolished the old house, it had to be, and when that was done the skunks were under there, and they all cut loose. It was pretty bad. Yet, there was never any odor in that house.

We discussed Nellie's personality on several occasions.

> For the holidays I took her meals for at least two meals. She loved pie. She loved her lemon pie, so I would take her a big half of lemon pie, and tell her she could have one that day and one the next, and I'd ask her the next time. Did you pay attention, Iris, "yeah, I ate one piece before midnight and one piece immediately after midnight."

> Oh, she had some nice clothes, she dressed well. She had some clothes here that still had the tags on them. She'd never even worn them. Of course, they were old fashioned by the time I knew her.

> She was good at supporting charities, she gave. She didn't go to church, however.

> She was very, very pleasant to be around.

I believe from what I have learned that she ran a good establishment.

> She was very careful too, you know. You have to know who you are letting in. She had five doors to that house, and they all had big padlocks on them. She was a good business woman, and she knew men.

She was aware of drugs, and she said that she never had taken them.

> I don't think Iris ever used any kind of drugs. I really don't think she would have allowed one of her girls to.

> She held tight reins on those girls. She also had a doctor down there every month to check those girls. Any time

one of them was sick or anything, she had a doctor immediately.

The girls lived in the house. There were several rooms in that house. The house was getting old; I don't know how old the house was. But some of the back rooms, the floors were beginning to fall in.

You mentioned to me that Nellie told you to check out all her clothes because she had money in them.

Right, she said she had a habit of putting $100 bills or a bunch of money in the lining. I always checked them before I did anything with them, I'd check them, but I never found any money ever.

How tall was Nellie?

She must have been about 5' 4", possibly 5' 5," when she was younger. She could have been 5'6," of course. I'm only 5'1", so most people are taller.

Do you know if she trusted banks?

Not a whole lot. However, she had a safety deposit box in the Bank of Durango and the First National Bank and Durango Savings and Loan, I believe.

******

Melissa Vance was a nurse's aid at the Four Corners Health Care for part of the time Nellie Spencer lived there. In April 1984, she discussed Nellie and her days as a patient.

Nellie kept to herself, never really talked to many of the people. I assumed much of it had to do with her hearing problems. She was one of the very few who did not have to get out of bed in the mornings. Part of that was because she paid her own way, and they tend to treat people with private money funds a little better.

She was very routine, very routine. She would ask you for a cup of coffee, and she would treat you then as a waitress, so to say. Really nice, it was real nice.

She was slow waking up. She would turn her radio and TV on, but not like she was paying attention to it. Perhaps it was not loud enough for her to hear. If it was it was too loud for the other patients.

Then she went through this routine of exercising every day, every day. She would do a little of it at night before going to bed. The whole routine was to make her body look pretty, her skin to look pretty. She did these exercises; she just hated fat women's legs. So she would go through this whole routine exercising her legs and her arms.

She would also get a damp cloth and put it over her face so her facial skin would look nice and not so many wrinkles would form, for a good fifteen to twenty minutes. Which was amazing, because you saw how she dressed up? She basically wore the same raggedy robe for the whole day. She just tore a rag and put it in her hair for a ribbon. But underneath she wanted to look nice. Every day, even when she was real sick, she would go through that routine.

It was interesting. During my time there we had some amazing aggressive men. Those men were always put at Nellie's table. She could handle them. We had a couple shipped off to the state hospital, she did great with them. I sensed she knew where her place was and when to talk and when not to, and that kind of thing. There were men always at her table.

As far as I remember, there were never any women there, and our prissiest women were seated the farthest away. I think it was part of the director's job setting it up. I felt there was an undertone of what Nellie used to be.

She really enjoyed her meals. She took her time and ate like she was in an elegant dining room. When I first met her, she took a glass of wine in the evening. She was also using a magnifying glass and reading cowboy westerns.

Nellie would relate to male nurses' aids much more than women's nurses aids. They just made over the women and the women loved it. They needed that kind of attention.

She said to me, "honey I know you have to do it," after she discussed the scheduling and other problems. She seemed to understand your position and was absolutely marvelous about it.

Nellie used to really work at getting people to laugh. She got really depressed when she realized her legs were getting tired and didn't work as well. Yet she really pushed herself to the maximum walking. When she saw herself breaking (health issues, plus age), she worried about it and got depressed.

What about the vinegar douche you mentioned?

> One time, when I was working the night shift, she talked more. I was complaining about the methods of birth control. I guess I asked her about what the women used to use. That's when she told me about that, and I felt that was a real special time, sort of a mother/daughter relationship. She said women used vinegar douches, she didn't talk a whole lot—she just said that's what she used and had her girls use.

> Nellie would tell you she had a really good life. She would light up, grin and smile and say that as if she had no regrets.

******

Longtime Durango resident, Dr. Leo Lloyd, came to know Nellie from another perspective, as the county physician. Along the way, Dr. Lloyd learned a great deal about the "oldest profession." He was interviewed on several occasions about Durango and its people – this time on September 15, 1983.

> Well, I came here in 1937. It was the duty of the county physician at that time. Since prostitution was allowed, the city council must have passed a resolution that they be examined once a month by the county physician, and that a notice be put in their rooms that they had been examined. And I made this expression, "clean as the driven snow" (laughed).

> So this was my duty, and I would call, get a hold of the madam, who was Nellie, and have her make an

appointment to send a girl up whenever she was due to come. As you may imagine, the examination was a very cursory exam – namely, interrogating the prostitute relative to symptoms of urinary burning or discharge and abdominal pain, or with a speculum and then take a smear of any secretion. I would do this once a month and then write on the prescription blank that I had seen Donna or whatever her name and examined her and found her free from all contagious diseases. It was a big statement to make, but it sufficed and she took it home and tacked it on the wall. I've seen it on the wall of their places, because I've been called down there. The next month she would return again.

As you can imagine in 1937, up until 1938, you could do all this but you couldn't do anything about it. There was no therapy, there were no antibiotics. In 1938 sulfanilamide came out, and we thought this would cure all gonorrhea and it helped. But penicillin, which came out in 1942, was more specific, and they were treated with penicillin.

Regarding Nellie, she ran a pretty tight ship, I felt she must. I had gone down here to look around and talked to her. She asked if I would come if she got into trouble at night. Her trouble at night was usually at the Fiesta or holiday season, and it was the trouble of men fighting over which woman they could have and drinking and fighting and creating havoc. These women seemed to be more emotional than the average individual. They weren't as stoic as you would think they might be.

Then all of them started scratching, fighting and yelling, it was quite a bit of commotion. Strangely enough the appearance of a doctor in the midst of this chaos had a great quieting effect. She didn't want the police down there so she called her doctor. And I had no (authority), if someone had walked in there with a gun, God knows what would have happened, because there were people in there with guns.

So she stayed away from the law and she called her friendly doctor. And I would come in and tell them to quiet down, and by that time there would be men scampering out here and there—some members of the city council, some other prominent individuals in town. By the time they all got out, the girls all quieted down, went to bed and they didn't do anymore work that night. She was very grateful, I think I was paid $5 a call for going down and paid $3 a call to examine the girls when they would come in monthly.

Of course the girls drank, and everybody was hard at it by the time I got down there. It was an experience for me, I've never dealt with that segment of the population before or since.

I never had any relationship with prostitution anywhere but here. They were extremely submissive and easy to deal with. For instance, they always ate at the Mandarin Café. The Canton and the Mandarin were next to one another, run by the Wongs. Mary (my wife) and I would often eat at the Mandarin and these girls would come in, filing into eat, and they would always eat at the back. As they came in, I never saw one turn her head toward me (in recognition). Mary knew all about this, and I would tell her, "here they come," and she was interested in seeing who those people were. They were decent individuals, and furthermore they paid their bills. They paid them in silver dollars.

There was nothing vulgar about these people from my relationship with them. There was trouble every fall when the Fiesta started, and the activities of (horse) racing, because a group of women who started out at Alamosa, then went to Monte Vista—Sky High Stampede—would come over here. The town was uncontrolled, whatever control was exercised was debatable.

They always paid their bills, came in with a sack of dollars, paid it in silver dollars. I felt it is a pretty hard way to make a living, but in (my) dealing with people outside, I've seen a lot worse, I'll say that.

Nellie was tough, she saw to it that they stayed in line. There was a great deal of jealousy about which man they would get, because they apparently got a little more on the side that they did not have to give to her. There was a lot of jealousy if the right person came in, they went overboard trying to please him.

I think that Nellie's place, as well as she could do it, was clean. She ruled with an iron fist. She was clever; she wasn't interested in the police at all. No matter what degree of trouble she got into, she didn't want to see policemen there.

That's why she called her doctor?

> The examination was imposed by the madam originally to keep herself out of trouble. Somebody would say something to her about "what shape were these girls in." She'd respond, well, here, this great doctor has given us a statement. It was ludicrous, but it was the only thing you could do. You're pure as the driven snow now, but not in five minutes.

> Nellie was married, and I wish I could remember the name. The man she married was a short little man who drank most of the time and really didn't do anything. He spent a good deal of his time (he was a veteran of WWI) in the VFW. If any event occurred, she would show up with him. They were accepted.

Would most people in town have known what Nellie did for an occupation?

> Oh, yes, I'm sure it was known. I'm sure it was discussed at every sewing circle, bridge club, and (along with) everything else, it was talked about. The interesting thing is the number of men of consequence in town who frequented the place. On several occasions, I saw people come out of there that I just couldn't believe. It was interesting to me as I look back on it. These people had a certain element of decency, and they could handle themselves pretty well out with people. On a number of occasions, Mary and I encountered these girls, and they never moved an eye.

Nellie had no misgiving about her life, at least I never thought so. She enjoyed what was going on, sure she did. I don't know who she serviced or anything about that; she was running the show when I got down there, running it with an iron hand.

Nellie always claimed she never caught anything.

They didn't know if they came down with anything, and a good deal of the time we didn't either. Maybe she didn't know, and many women had gonorrhea in a very mild form, others were desperately sick.

Did you use mercury to treat the women? I heard once that the old saying went like this, "thirty seconds with Venus and a lifetime of mercury."

Our treatment was made up mainly with arsenic and bismuth. I don't remember if I used mercury. Mercury was so terribly toxic. What we used was an improvement over mercury. At its best, it was a most disheartening thing, because the treatment was almost worse than the disease. I mean the side effects. Most people wouldn't keep coming. People don't change. They won't keep coming back usually, if it was going to take a long while.

Then Dr. Lloyd went on to say:

That, of course, was not where all the prostitution was. A good share of it was in the south end of 6th Street. When the Southern Hotel was active—present parking lot across from the depot—it was a place where almost exclusively cattlemen, sheepmen would come in on the railroad to buy or sell stock. They would check in at the

Southern, which was a very hospitable hotel. In fact, they didn't have the worse food, they had liquor and they had women. So everything these men wanted was there, and they didn't have to leave the building. Others knew the girls down by the river.

There was one lone girl in the area between where the COD laundry used to be and the red house (1499 block of Main), who operated there by herself. She lived there under pretty miserable conditions—there was no sanitation, just not the best.

******

Two other Durangoans, as young boys, recalled their contacts and their experiences with the Red Light District and its denizens.

I used to deliver the **Durango Democrat** on the Main Street Route that included the red light district, toward the river from Main Street. My grandmother, a very lovely Swedish person, said, "Herbert don't ever go into those little houses on the river side of Main Street"—to which I replied, "why, grandma, those girls are my best friends and I see them every morning and they pay right on time."

While I was in high school, I used to work at Parsons Drug Store and later at a grocery store. Betty Hickey would call the orders in, and I would take them down to her house. The druggist always had the order wrapped, so I never knew what I was carrying. The tips were real good, but I was told not to inquire what went on there. If I did, I would be fired. Boys before had been fired for breaking that rule. It turned out to be the best job I had. She had a neon sign over her place; it just said "Betty's." It was hard to miss down there along the river. Betty closed the establishment and left town, to where I don't know.

I once briefly talked to one of Nellie's clients who, by the time I talked to him, was married. His short comments told much about her and her skills. "Nellie was a great lay. The best sex I ever had."

Nellie, Bessie, and Friends
Durango's Queens of the
Tenderloin

The red light district remained part of life for Durango and Durangoans, well into the twentieth century. Locals viewed it from a variety of perspectives and attitudes. Over the years, I fortunately was able to interview several who appear in this chapter, covering a range of subjects relating to their community. Among the topics about which I inquired, or they simply started discussing, were the district and its girls. The following are interviews recounting memories of a now vanished time and institution.

Iris (Nellie) was not alone among the girls remembered working in Durango. Two madams were recalled in particular, Bessie Rivers, who along with her sister, had arrived in the town in the early 1880s, and Betty Hickey, who appeared in the mid-1920s.

I interviewed Marguerite Cantrell on December 1, 1977. Marguerite (born 1897) was the daughter of Harry Jackson, a pioneer Durango hardware merchant. Her father had been one of the "prime movers" in the community's early history and had established Jackson Hardware.

Jackie Nixon
Courtesy Duane A. Smith

Did you know Bessie Rivers?

Yes, very well. She used to come into the store. She was a big woman, nice looking, always dressed nice. She would come into the store to buy something and the girl that was waiting on customers—and even some of the young men— didn't want to wait on her. So, one day, my father told me to be as nice to her as I can. I didn't know who she was. She was very nice to me. When she left, Pop told me who she was, the girl who has the red light district, the lady of the red light district. (He said) "A lot of people didn't like to have her come in the store or bring her girls in, nor did they like to wait on her. Don't you ever be that way. Her money is part of our bread and butter." After that, every time she came in she would ask for me.

She used to have one of the old fashioned phaetons. You could see a person's whole body, so to speak. It was a buggy, front seat and back seat, you step right into it. She used to dress her girls up, four beautiful, beautiful girls and parade up and down Main Street. I didn't know who in the world it was, this was when I was very young, and I used to watch those girls. They were so lovely, and they had their big hats on, their umbrellas, and one or two of them would be smoking, which you didn't do in those days. Ladies didn't. I finally said to my mother: "why does that lady smoke, and why does that lady take those beautiful girls out and in the street?" I don't know how she answered me, I don't know how she could. But it was quite a sight.

Bessie had that big house by the Silver Spur (on Main Avenue in Animas City). She moved out there after she discontinued having the other type of house and more or less retired, when she went out there.

******

Lester Gardenswartz first arrived in Durango in 1916 and eventually opened a sporting goods store on Main Street in September, 1928. He was interviewed on January 14 and May 17, 1977.

I ran across, of all things, in my research, a bond that you co-signed for Betty Hickey. What type of a person was Betty?

Well, as you know, she ran a sporting house, but she was a very fine lady; she was a perfect lady, regardless of her line of business. Her word was the same thing as her bond. To me and to my wife, who knew her real well, she was a fine lady—it was her work, of course, that put a lot of people's noses up in the air. But she got into a little trouble here in town over a car, and I and another fellow here in town signed her bond until she got it straightened out. She used to advertise, just kidding me, the only bonded sporting house in America.

She called it a whorehouse, pardon me. The only bonded whorehouse in America. As a joke, you know. But she had to appear in court one day; we all had to appear. (Leonard Glazer was the other man who signed the note.) So I called her one day to tell her that we had to be in court at 10:00, and I must have woke her up. She said, "God-danged you, Gardenswartz, don't you know we work all night and sleep all day." I'll never forget that as long as I live. But she would come in the store during the day and say, "let's go for a coke or something," and my wife and I would go out with her to have a coke, sit with her and talk over events of the day, just like you would with anyone else. She was a very fine lady.

When did she come to Durango?

She came in about 1925 or 1926, and she had a house of about four girls, and they were all beautiful girls—I mean she ran a nice clean place, she really did, considering the business she was in.

She left then (in World War II) and joined the WACs or the WAVES, I don't know which. And she came down here on a furlough, and I took her down to the Lions Club, and she gave the program on the girls in the service. She was a captain, and they picked the right one, because she knew how to handle women.

She didn't come back then, after the war, did she?

We lost track of her, and I don't know whatever happened. She never came back. That was Betty Hickey.

There was Frances Belmont up at Silverton that was a very fine lady who ran a sporting house, and she was good to us when we were getting started. She had a house with a bar in the front and a pool table, and she would let us put out our wares for miners' paydays. Like we would take a few guns up and a few watches— anything to make a living if we could sell it. She let us use her place. She was very good to my brother Sam and me.

Betty seemed to have been well liked in town.

Ah, well, Betty was a very fine lady. I know my wife felt a little embarrassed by going out with a lady that ran a sporting house, but we became very good friends, as far as going out for a coke and talking over the events of the day.

We thought nothing of it, being seen with her. In my book she was a fine lady. In my book, she was a fine woman.

✶✶✶✶✶✶

Dr. Leo Lloyd, who commented on Nellie Spencer in Chapter 7, came to Durango in 1936 and practiced medicine there (except during World War II, when he went into service) until he retired. This interview took place on November 8, 1976.

When I came here in 1936, I was appointed county physician, and we had a lot of prostitutes here. At the very end of Main Street, across from the train station, there is an open parking space there now. That was the site of the Southern Hotel. The hotel was owned by Angelo Dallabetta, and I'm not sure Angelo would like to be related to this necessarily. Angelo ran a pretty-free going house, mainly a man's hotel.

People would come in on the train, sheepmen in for a weekend or a week. Cattlemen would come in and bring their cattle and stay here and stay at the Southern. And he had four or five girls, all the time in there. Next door to that there was a saloon and upstairs, above the saloon, there were two women. And then behind the site of the COD Laundry (1177 Main Avenue), along the railroad track, were four little, single room houses where girls operated individually in there. And then, down on the bank of the river, the house is still down there, was Betty's place, which had about five girls. (It was located near the site of the present Riverside City Hall in Iris Park The house is now gone, but a historical marker tells its tale and Nellie's as well.)

That was Betty's place. And Betty later joined the army and became a WAC incidentally. She knew how to handle women so well. But one of the duties of the county physician was to examine the prostitutes every month; to be sure they were as pure as the driven snow. So Dr. Martin (his partner) and I took care of them, and they were really a credible bunch of girls. They were decent, they came into the office, they were never "unlady-like"…they were very quiet people. And we did examinations for gonorrhea and syphilis and gave them a slip that they'd been examined, which they put up in their room. Which of course is a stupid thing, because five minutes after they left, you know, they could have been infected by anybody.

The town didn't have a law for prostitution, but it was such an arrangement that the City Council thought they're here, nobody really wants to get rid of them. So why don't we ask the county physician to just sort of supervise them, which we did.

And then, of course, in the summer, when the Fiesta came along and the rodeo, why they would import eight or ten girls from Alamosa. And the place would be full down there, and we would check them out too.

I remember when Mary (my wife) and I would go out to eat, if we'd go to the Strater Hotel, they would sometimes be there. They would go anywhere. They always stayed on the west side of Main (900 block, where the saloons were located). Really, it was a rule at that time that the ladies of the town would walk on the east side of Main (900 block) and not the other side. (The exception was the First National Bank, which was on the west corner of 9th and Main.) Other people would walk on the west side, and they (the girls) would eat in the restaurants, however.

They used to pay us in silver dollars for everything. When we'd operated on one of them, they'd come with a bagful of silver dollars and plunk it down. And we took care of them. Interestingly enough, they were allowed (to conduct business) because many of the important people in town used them, including members of the City Council.

What finally closed them down here in Durango?

They left. There was a lot of criticism in the paper about them. People began writing letters, and they just sort of drifted away. This was probably in 1950. I had nothing to do with these women, as far as examining them and then requiring any slips, after 1946-47. It was all in the earlier days.

What happened to Betty Hickey?

I don't know what happened to Betty. Many of us often talked about her. She was quite a character. She knew men probably better than almost anybody. She also knew women and knew the volatile situation and their reaction to the real stress of a bunch of drunken men dropping in and demanding this and that. The girls used to just go crazy. There were some pretty wild events down there, I recall. Late at night, fellas would come in, drinking and fighting over a certain girl.

I was amazed at who I saw running out of there, cause it really was an interesting thing. But I could understand then why they were allowed, because people of some stature in the town wanted it.

******

Richard Macomb grew up in Durango, and entered the banking business. He was interviewed on August 25, 1977.

I did not know that you had ever met Bessie Rivers. What type of a person was she?

> She was cute, yeah, she was a pretty woman. She was very good looking in her younger days. She was a rather large woman. She was fairly heavy, and she was fairly tall. I would say about 5' 9" tall. She had maybe six or eight girls working for her, and she would tell Mr. Parsons (Parsons Drug Store), when I was at Parsons, that if she wanted to charge to these girls that she would stand good for it. We did quite a little of that, charged, and, by gosh, those people were the best payers you ever seen. I don't think we ever called on her. She saw to it and their word was good, you never had to call her. Their word was good—it was law to them. They said they would pay it, and, by gosh, they would pay it. She ran a very respectable place. She was in it to make money. They would sell beer for $1 a bottle.

******

Dentist Schulyer Parker arrived in Durango in 1925 to start his practice. He was interviewed November 18, 1976.

When I came here, there was a regular district west of the tracks, between the tracks and the river, say in the 1000 and 1100 block down in there. They were shacks, some of those gals had been here for a long time; they were known by everybody. There was a woman who owned a home out in Animas City, name of Bessie Rivers. Everybody in this area knew about Bessie Rivers, and she lived upstairs over the Mandarin Café in her old age. I never met her.

I remember seeing Betty Hickey in Parsons Drug store one time. She was a good looking woman. That was a very interesting chapter of Durango. Every town, mining town of this sort, had their red light district. You can't do away with prostitution or gambling either one.

This is just a personal observation, but I think we ought to have our red light districts now. It would go a long ways towards doing away with a lot of our crimes that are committed today—sex crimes—and all kinds of things.

******

Gilbert Lujan's folks moved to Durango about 1933. He worked at Fort Lewis College and was interviewed on August 16, 1977.

My folks moved down below the railroad tracks behind the laundry (COD)—that was where they had the prostitutes, three or four houses. And to separate the people, they built fences, high fences, so we couldn't see what was going on. Of course, it was no problem, you know how kids are.

As a matter of fact, I got a job hauling water and wood for those women. They treated me nice; they were good women really. Nothing out of the way when I was working there. Of course, I knew what they did. The madam's name was Iris Spencer. We rented from her.

Most of the girls were—I don't know just how old, but young. All that I can remember were Anglos. With them women, activity went on until all hours of the morning. I don't know when those gals ever slept. There were people all over that damn place.

They were nice, they treated me nice. You know them women, I guess, they never ventured beyond that fence. Once in a while, you would see them go to town if they had to get something, but they were pretty well contained.

They used to burn wood. There were three rows of houses. The first row, two houses, and the second row, one house was theirs, then another row. And down by the river, there was another row and centrally located was a water pool. And this is what we hauled water form. Buckets for drinking water, washing clothes, etc. There was no running water in the houses. But, like I said, they treated me real nice, and they paid me. They were generous.

******

Deora Powell was born in Durango in June 1900. The wife of a coal miner, she was a midwife who eventually became a Licensed Practical Nurse. Deora was interviewed October 29, 1997 and August 6, 1998.

I knew Bessie Rivers. She was red light, but to everybody that ever went to her and talked to her, she was really good-hearted. They said that if a man needed a meal, she bought it for him.

Bessie Rivers was a real nice person. The only thing, we didn't have much to do with her, because my Dad was very strict. He didn't believe in letting us associate with anybody like that. We never was allowed below Main Street down there, you know.

A decent woman never walked up the west side of the 900 block of Main because there was nothing there but saloons and joints. They would come up to the First National Bank and then cross over.

Bessie Rivers was pretty heavy set, big heavy set woman, dark hair, but everybody that knew her and everything said that she was good-hearted, and if anybody was broke, she would help them out. She wasn't bad looking.

******

Housewife and clerk, Edna Goodman, also remembered Bessie Rivers. In a January 19, 1980 interview, she commented:

I tell you, when I was down at the store (Goodman's paint store) during the depression, she used to come in once in awhile, and she was very nice. I waited on her just like everyone else. I don't know anything about her, except coming in the store. Ladies didn't walk on the west side of Main Street, 900 block. I still have "reservations" about walking over there. I don't know why.

******

Leonard Glazer was born in Durango in July 1910 and lived in the community for nearly the rest of his life.

> There was a red light district down at the foot of 12th Street and westward across the railroad tracks. There were, oh, possibly at one time, eight to ten small houses. They were "shacky" houses. Finally, one of the occupants, her name was Iris Spencer, she and her husband eventually bought the area.
>
> She bought it and, about that time too, another gal came along by the name of Betty Hickey. And she talked Mrs. Spencer into letting her have the sole concession of the district. So, she took one of the houses and worked it over and modernized it and even piped natural gas over to the property where she could heat the house and also have hot water. And she operated that place until the war started. And, of course, when the war started, a lot of the young people left and Betty couldn't make a go of it, so she left too. But I knew her well, she was quite an individual and character.
>
> I always collected money from merchants for the Spanish Trails Fiesta. So I always collected from 12th Street southward to 9th Street. And one year I had finished my collections, and I was asked if I would pick up a couple of the places outside my district. I said I would, and Betty Hickey's House was one of them.
>
> So I went down there one afternoon at 4 p.m., and I knocked at the door. One of Betty's girls answered the

door for me and showed me inside. I told her that I was primarily down there to make a collection, to accept a contribution, for the Spanish Trails Fiesta. About that time she laid me low. She said, "You can take your Spanish Trails Fiesta and b-e-e-p it!" I said, "What's wrong?" She said,"A fellow came down here the other morning at seven to collect for the Fiesta and anybody ought to know better than to come at seven in the morning. We're not in business at seven o'clock in the morning."

So I talked to her and got her stabilized, and she said she'd have some money for me. So she did, she finally sent up a check. So she made a contribution to me. We were always real good friends. In fact, she never let anyone else collect for the Fiesta Committee.

Betty was possibly around forty. She had quite a confrontation with Iris Spencer and her husband, because she was supposed to have the sole concession down there. But she caught Iris going ahead and running a place herself. And she quit paying her rent; she was paying $150 a month for this old shacky house, which was a pretty good price in those days. So she was paying a good rent, and she discontinued it, and, before I knew, one day her attorney called me and said, "Betty's in trouble down there having a fight with Iris. We've got to help her out."

And I said, "What do you want me to do?" He said, "We're trying to get a bond set up between Betty and the Spencers on this rental deal. Would you consider signing it?" I said, "Oh, I guess so, I want to see how it reads before I do." And he did, and I went to his office and I said I'd sign. "It's written up so it didn't implicate me in making any payments if Betty don't. I was asked, "do you think that you could get somebody else to go on the bond with you?"

(The attorney suggested Lester Gardenswartz and Nate Stein and he asked Glazer to talk to them. He agreed.)

So I called them and they said, "We'll go on your recommendation." And I said, "It actually didn't bind us at all . . . . it's not worth the paper it's written on." And I told (Tommy Hatfield, the attorney) as long as the other attorney would accept it, it was alright with me. So the three of us signed the bond and put Betty back in good graces with the Spencers. It was quite humorous, word got around that we had bonded the only red light district in the U. S.

Would you go into more detail about Betty and her girls?

I don't think she ever had over, maybe, four or five girls. I would say none of them were any older than Betty, I would say they were from nineteen, twenty, on up. They were all Anglo girls.

Betty spent her money freely here, as long as she was making it. She always drove a good automobile, late model car. And there was never any rough housing that was ever conducted down at her place. She was never involved in any other type of crime. Nothing ever implicated her at all. The place was run on a good basis. There wasn't any bad situation having it in town. In fact,

I've said lots of times that the condition in those days was a lot better than it has been recently. The venereal disease situation wasn't like it is now. They kept it under control.

The city allowed her to operate. They gave her place protection when she needed it. It was located in the city; it was off to one side, so it never interfered with anybody at all. The situation just ran on, and it was a good condition for the town. It was better than in recent years, with these young girls trotting up and down as walkers in Durango.

You knew Bessie Rivers?

Bessie was a very high type person, a perfect lady. There was an area down in there where Bessie was (west of 10th Street). And later she moved up, and she bought the building that is where Johnson Jewelry was (965 Main Street). And she was upstairs over Johnson Jewelry, and she conducted a good place. Course, in those days, she sold some beer in her place. She later owned the white house over here at 33rd and Main. After Bessie passed away, a son came to Durango to take over her estate, and his name was Arthur Ferguson. He sold her property and then moved to where he was residing at the time.

She used to call me to come down, and she would always want me to deliver her insurance policies. And I would take them down to her. She'd write me a check right on the spot and pay me. She was a great (person), Bessie Rivers.

Another person whom Bessie was very friendly with, she was very fine to him and he was wonderful to her. His name was Charles A. Cooke. He was a professional gambler, and Charles looked after her just like he was married to her. He took her every day from her building to this house, which was then in Animas City. Charlie was very fine to Bessie, and she was to him. He was a real high class gambler.

******

On April 14, 1986, I interviewed Georgia Cook who grew up in nearby Ignacio when the red light district still was part of Durango.

> I lived in the country, was raised in the country. This other little friend of mine and some others were just scared to death coming to Durango for fear we would run into some of these ladies who might want us to go down to the row—the houses along where the Town Plaza now is and against the river.

> To tell the truth, after I was married, I met the main one and her name was Bessie Rivers. She was one of the sweetest women you ever met in your life. She would do anything for anybody to help them out. She lived up in Animas City, but Bessie was one of the swellest women you ever met.

Was she pretty?

> Yes, a lovely woman. She was a good woman, as good as gold with other people. She couldn't stand to see anyone go hungry or anything. She would see they

got something. She was a wonderful person. She had a sister who was an invalid. She purchased most of the books for her. (Georgia had purchased some of her books when they had a sale after her death.) Some of them were westerns, others were just good books.

Nor was it simply "old-timers" who had a positive view of Bessie Rivers. An undated news item (the week of December 19, 1909), which appeared in the seventy-five-year ago column in *Today* (December 19, 1984), stated:

> We don't see any church philanthropists busy, no one, but we sure saw one of the 'fallen women' scattering $5 bills. We know who received them, where they went, the beneficiaries needed every dollar that came their way. And Bessie Rivers opened her purse.

******

A gentleman, who wished to remain anonymous, was born in Durango in December, 1894, and described his formative years in the town in an undated 1985 letter.

> There was an area on Main Street called the Saloon Block. The west side was all saloons on the ground floor and basement, with roulette, faro, and other games of chance. No age limit, and high school kids would try and hit the Jack Pot. The ladies of Durango were never permitted by custom on that side of the street. Between Main Street and the river there were two-story gambling houses and saloons and from the railroad to the river were the cribs.

Some enterprising person set the whole street, both sides, afire one night. I recall going down after the fire, picking up poker chips. They were great to make whistles, being made of gutta-percha. We used to heat and bend them and put a small hole in the middle and it made a fine whistle.

An era ended with the closing of the last "parlor" house in the early 1950s. Those girls in the "back seats of automobiles" whom Nellie so despised, and free-lancers, plus those who gave it away "for free" (Nellie did not think much of them either), ended a time that had started back with the founding of the community. Public pressure, worrying about the effect the district had on young men's morals, and concern about Durango's image also aided in closing the district. Those who had long campaigned against the evil epitomized by the red light district and its "fair but frail" were at last victorious over such shocking sin.

Times had changed. Public attitudes had changed. The old West had vanished into legend. With it all, a part of Durango's history vanished. Now only tourists and others can read about it on historic signs and in books or visit a district with perhaps one of the houses turned into a museum.

Epilogue
Requiem for Prostitution

Bessie, Nellie, Betty, Pearl, and their "working girl" counterparts throughout the San Juans have long since become part of the past. It is an intriguing history for many people, both then and now, and to others, a demeaning and repelling story of the exploitation of women. In their own way, however, the "ladies of the line" were regarded as an indispensable part of a booming mining community. Even during the Victorian era, an era of nearly inflexible sexual moral standards, prostitution existed as part of the culture despite public anguish regarding its sinful nature. It might have existed out of sight, "on the other side of the tracks," but it existed.

Notwithstanding those accounts that looked at the bleakness of the occupation, even moralizing against it, these same accounts often found a glimpse of a seemingly zestful life style. Nonetheless, it proved a demoralizing, dangerous, and generally dead-end occupation for the women involved, whether they worked in a lowly crib or the most high-class parlor house.

Nellie entered the "business" at a time when prostitution was changing throughout the West. With prohibition and the generally successful attempts to close the red light districts, prostitution had changed from the high rolling times of a generation earlier. Vice moved underground, so to speak. Lodging houses and "low class" hotels, plus "rustling" on the street, came to replace the parlor houses and cribs. Prostitutes demonstrated a persistence and flexibility in pursuit of their trade. The demimonde did not disappear, as Nellie's career well illustrated.

A tendency to glamorize prostitution appears in popular westerns. Along with this, the glorification of the prostitute in recounting the boom days of "long ago" in some western communities has tended to distort reality. To return to Anne Butler and her *Sisters of Joy,* the realistic story emerges.

> Prostitutes came from among the poorest groups of women on the frontier. They were the daughters of cultures where servitude had taken a toll. Such women turned to prostitution at an early age and entered the profession with few skills and only rudimentary education. They brought little that would help them alter lives marked by ignorance and impoverishment....
>
> In an arena of unchecked competition, the economic rewards proved marginal. Most prostitutes did not earn substantial sums, mainly because they drew their clientele from among other workers with little money. (pp. 150-51)

Nellie certainly fit the pattern stated in the first paragraph. She was a daughter of poverty, with minimal education, and she entered the profession at an early age. She did, however, deviate from the observations made in the second paragraph. Perhaps it was due to her natural business ability, sheer luck, the changing times, or a higher class of clientele. Still it remains difficult to determine; although having known her, I would lean toward her innate business ability. Without doubt, she enjoyed the money she made and handled it very well through her investments and savings.

She also witnessed and experienced the other side of the business. There existed a bleakness, a desperation, and the stigma of living on the "wrong side of the tracks." A degradation of women associated with prostitution existed, and it should not be dismissed as romantic, exciting, or a road to fortune. The strain – physically, emotionally, and mentally – must have been draining, as was certainly shown by the short tenure in the business for most of the girls. The threat of arrest, the occurrence of violence, the prevalence of alcohol, the temptation of drugs, the potential for disease, the variety of clientele, and their social outcast status left the women debilitated and aged beyond their time. There seemed no way out for most, despite the legends and fantasies.

The reality of prostitution was shown in a variety of ways, but no more so than in the sadly recurrent notices of suicides or attempted suicides by the girls. That local papers often made light of the event perhaps says more than was intended by the reporter or appreciated and understood by the readers. More likely than not, however, the notice moralized on a life gone astray.

Young Mabel Barbee's fantasy about the beautiful and dashing Pearl De Vere came to a tragic end in this manner on Christmas Eve. The *Cripple Creek Times* simply reported, "Pearl De Vere, madam at the Old Homestead, died early today from an overdoes of morphine." Mabel described it, in her *Cripple Creek Days,* as "the saddest Christmas of my life."

Mabel decided to visit the mortuary. "Several days passed before I could muster sufficient courage to take such a bold step," she anguished.

I leaned over the coffin for a better view. She looked so
natural that she might have opened her eyes and smiled

up at me slantwise through her long lashes. If there had been any strain of wickedness in her face Death had erased it ....(She went to the cemetery for the funeral.) All at once, through a break in the ranks, I caught a glimpse of the flower-laden casket being lowered into the ground and then came the sad sweet notes of Joe Moore's cornet playing 'Good-by, Little Girl, Good-Bye.' That was too much for me to bear; my heart was broken and I buried my face in my coat and sobbed ....
I felt suddenly weary, older and more grown up.

In the course of so short a time, Mabel Barbee had seen both the romance and the tragedy of the "heroine of my fondest daydreams."

Yet she still witnessed only part of the story. The medical problems associated with prostitution, affecting both the seller and the buyer, cannot be simply dismissed as incidental. Syphilis and related social diseases had no known full-fledged cure. Either party might have the "curse." All that the so-called patent medicine cures accomplished was to mask the symptoms. Tragically, innocent women could also fall victim to these diseases after their husbands, in their "wild" youth, had visited the line. Sadly, that could lead to medical problems for their children as well.

The effects of prostitution also had a tendency to corrupt those who came in contact with it, including both the local government and local law enforcement agencies. It took hours of council member and police time to regulate, answer citizen concerns, and tend to other business related to the district and its inhabitants. The red light district also proved to be a financial drain on the San Juan towns and other communities. There can be no question, however, that town governments profited from the monthly fines and additional payments reaped from prostitution. Whether a gain or loss to the town's treasury was realized will never be known, however the additional revenue probably matched the additional expenses.

That this tie between local government and the district existed cannot be doubted. In her book, *Red Light Women of the Rocky Mountains,* Jan MacKell concluded:

> A business relationship between prostitution and government began when authorities figured out that they too could make money from the sex trade. Fines, fees, and licenses filled city hall safes, although authorities often wondered if this largesse was worth the violence, thievery, and tragedy that accompanied it.

Add to this, the kickbacks and bribes to local law enforcement—and even to the city fathers—and one can begin to see why prostitution might not be a profitable enterprise or even a marginal business.

There can be no question, though, that prostitution was embodied as an integral part, one might be tempted to say essential part, of the life and times of the San Juan mining era. As one shocked observer of the wide-open bordellos noted, mining camps "openly wear their worse side out." To many observers, prostitution led to a career of "debauchery, drunkenness and all-around dissipation," as an 1899-1900 report of the *Colorado Bureau of Labor Statistics* claimed.

In this masculine world, though, it provided an essential element of the social life and to a degree the economic life of the communities and mining districts. Even the contention that a camp or town without a red light district was no community at all supports that image and buttresses the reality. However it should not be assumed, as has been mentioned earlier, that this pattern was isolated to the late nineteenth and early twentieth century San Juans or Colorado. Districts were found elsewhere throughout the country where similar conditions existed, offering few reputable outlets for women to make a respectable living through their own efforts. In the masculine-dominated world around them, women were second class citizens.

One of the questions I hoped to resolve during the interviews was: did Nellie enjoy her occupation? From most of her answers it would seem to be that she did. Such comments touting a "good free life," enjoying the money she made, and the numerous times she mentioned "we had fun" do not seem to have been simply a rote memory of something she did solely for financial reward. Nellie might be said to have been a sexually liberated woman slightly ahead of her time.

All that aside however, as Nellie admitted, if she had to do it all over again, she would have settled down into a more respectable married life. Whether such an attitude would have prevailed among other prostitutes cannot be known. In the end, no matter what one may think of Bessie, Nellie, Pearl, or Betty, they were part of the history of their times and deserve their chance to stand at history's bar and tell their story. As Anne Butler concluded, "Prostitutes made contributions to the emergence of that western society; that their contributions appear less 'good' or 'noble' does not make them less important." (p. 155)

The era in which Nellie and her "sisters in sin" lived and worked was, indeed, a more earthy time than the present. However, in this twenty-first century, the "oldest profession" lives on, changed in approach, to be sure, but not in basic desires and services offered. In the words of the unknown writer of the book of *Ecclesiastes*:

> For everything there is a season
> and a time for every matter under heaven:
>
> A time to be born, and a time to die…
> a time to break down, and a time to build up;
> a time to weep, and a time to laugh;
> a time to mourn, and a time to dance:
> a time to seek, and a time to lose;
> a time to keep silence, and a time to speak;
> a time to love, and a time to hate;
> a time for war, and a time for peace.

This has been a story that encompasses almost all of that. It cannot be changed. Because the telling might lead to a better understanding of a misunderstood way of life, for Nellie, at least, it was "a time to speak."

Index

Aspen, 30

Baker, Charles, 2
Bancroft, Hubert Howe, 4
Belmont, Frances, 123, 125
Blacks, 58
Breunig, Lara, 70-71
Bronco Lou, 36
Butler, Anne, 142, 146
Byers, William, 6, 8

Cantrell, Marguerita, 121
Chase, Clara, 44
Chinese, 40-41
Columbia, 24-25
Cook, Georgia, 137
Creede, 12, 13, 25-26, 27, 48, 57, 62
Cripple Creek, 54
Cusey, Mildred, x-xi

Dallabetta, Angelo, 126
Dance Houses, 18, 21
Darley, George, 34-35
Day, David, 37, 41-42, 44
Day, Victoria, 42
DeVere, Pearl, ii-iii, 143-44
Denver, 79, 81
Denver& Rio Grande Railroad, 5
Diseases, 77, 91-92, 112-14, 117. 144
Doctors, 91

Durango, 1, 13, 14, 21, 27-28, 29, 38, 52, 82-83

Fossett, Frank, viii, 3

Gardenswartz, Lester, 123, 135
Glazer, Leonard, 133
Goodman, Edna, 132
Grand Junction, 86

Hartman,Magg,34
Hickey, Betty, 37, 121, 123-25, 126-27, 128, 131, 132
Hoffman, Ernest, ix-x
Howardsville, 9

Jacobson, Ellen, viii

Lake City, 7, 20-21, 38
Lannell, Carrie, 42
Leadville, 33-34. 80-81
Lee, Mabel Barbee, ii, 143
Lewis, Nettie, 41
Lindsay, Vera, 103
Livermore, Robert, 54
Lloyd, Leo, 112, 126
Lloyd, Mary, 127-28
Lujan, Gilbert, 130

MacKell, Jan, iv, 145

Macomb, Richard, 129
Martin, Christopher, 127
Marsh, Grace, 41
McCoy, Belle, 37
Mears, Otto, 2, 10
Meeker (town), 65-66, 67
Meeker, Nathan, 3, 66
Miller, Margaret, 49
Morris, Mary, 82

Ophir, 37
Opium, 40
Ouray, 10, 23-24, 38, 50, 56, 62

Packer, Alferd, 7
Parker, Schulyer, 129
Pets, 96
Police, 87
Powell, Deora, 131
Pregnancy, 88
Prohibition, 62
Prostitution, San Juans. See
        Chapters, 2, 3, 4

Rico, 11, 22-23
Rivers, Bessie, 121-23, 137-38
Romney, Caroline, 38-39, 92
Rothschild, Maggie, 36

Silverton, ix-x, 8, 9, 17, 18-19, 57
Smith, Jefferson "Soapy," 48
Smith, Sarah, 39
Spanish Trails Fiesta, 133
Spencer, Herbert, 70, 104
Suicide, 99, 143

Telluride, viii-ix, 12, 24-25, 30, 52, 56
Town Government. See individual
        towns

Twain, Mark, xi, 33

Urbanization, 1-2, 6. See chapters,
        2-4
Utes, 3

Vance, Melissa, 109
Virginia City, Nevada, xi

Woman's Christian Temperance
        Union, 60
Wommach, Linda, v